Stephanie

Explore

Step Yowell

JS

7/09   10-
8-07

Jan lewis

Praise for *The Hippie Guide to Climbing the Corporate Ladder & Other Mountains*

"I wish this enlightening book had been available 30 years ago. The inspiration I have derived from it now would have been welcomed then. Like a new band without a 'label' (either style or record company), with originality and dedication it shows how they forged their own way and set the high marks for others to strive for. This 'how it was done' book should be read by all aspiring musicians, for the principles of success are universal and are defined within."

—John McEuen, Founding member of Nitty Gritty Dirt Band (also celebrating our 40th year!) and father of 6 kids who could not wear out their JanSport packs

"Skip's account of the founding of JanSport is full of honesty, humor, and enough anecdotes to stir a memory in almost anyone who has spent time outside. His tale takes you from a small room above a transmission shop to a global enterprise and packs enough adventures to keep the fire stoked and the beer on ice for hours."

—Larry Burke, Editor-in-Chief, *Outside* Magazine

"This is by far the most entertaining business book I've ever encountered! During the entire read, I felt as if I were sitting at a camp on a faraway mountain swapping stories with Skip. He has filled his book with real world wisdom on how to build a business grounded in authenticity and meaningfulness."

—Doug Hall, CEO Eureka! Ranch, Author of the *Jump Start Your Business Brain*, "Truthteller" Judge on ABC TV's *American Inventor*

"This amazing book chronicles the life of Skip Yowell, a man who climbed the corporate ladder not in a suit and tie, but in hiking boots and with a backpack. He did so in style, and had tons of fun doing it. He stayed true to himself, maintained friendships, traveled the world and most importantly, preserved his passion for his job.

We can all learn something from Skip, who started building backpacks from scratch and created a company that is now a giant in the industry. His honesty and passion for life are his priority, which all of his friends and business associates can attest to. The world would be a better place with more people like Skip Yowell. I am proud to have him as my friend and encourage you to get to know his story! You'll be inspired."

> —Ed Viesturs, First American to climb all fourteen 8,000 meter peaks, Author of *No Shortcuts to the Top*

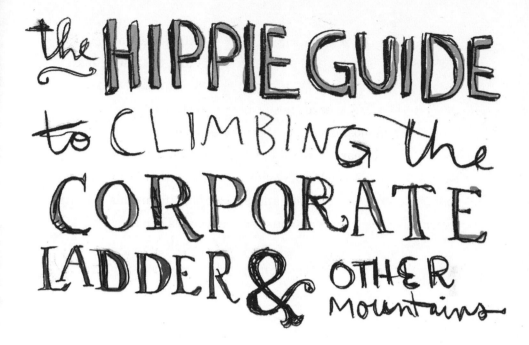

the HIPPIE GUIDE
to CLIMBING the
CORPORATE
LADDER & OTHER Mountains

HOW JANSPORT
makes it HAPPEN

SKIP YOWELL
CO-founder of JANSPORT

NAKED
INK

Published in Nashville, Tennessee, by NAKED INK™, a division of the General Trade Book Group of Thomas Nelson Publishers, Inc. Please visit us at www.nakedink.net.

Library of Congress Cataloging-in-Publication data on file with the Library of Congress.

ISBN 10: 1-59555-852-7
ISBN 13: 978-1-59555-852-7

Printed in the United States of America
06 07 08 09 10 — 5 4 3 2 1

THIS BOOK IS DEDICATED TO:

Winnie Kingsbury

Quinn Yowell

Drew Kingsbury

CONTENTS

FOREWORD
BY PETER JENKINS

*I*t was 1984 but it looked like it could have been 1684.

If another yak caravan came through the village of Xegar, our view of the world's tallest mountains would be cut off by clouds of dust. Skip Yowell and I were on one of our many adventures. This time we were winding our way through Tibet on our way to Mt. Everest.

In front of us, a small boy was standing on a wall made of stone and mud flying a hand-built kite. I heard the jingle of bells— a familiar sound in these mountain valleys and narrow rock- cluttered passes. The yaks were lumbering along at typical yak-speed, flicking their tails as they moved towards us.

The nomad leading the caravan had most likely been up in the mountain meadows all summer, away from his home village. A long turquoise earring dangled in bold contrast against his dark, weathered skin. He walked slowly with his hands clasped behind his back. His hands were blackened from the yak dung he used as fuel for the fires that heated both his body and his yak-butter tea. Although this journey may have already taken the yak herder a month, time did not seem to matter here in these mountains like it does everywhere else I have ever been.

The reason Skip and I were here was that JanSport was sponsoring an elite team of US mountain climbers on the China-Everest '84 expedition, led by famed mountaineer, Lou Whitaker. Lou's twin brother, Jim, was the first American to summit Mt. Everest back in 1963. Like most of the other climbers before him, he ascended from the Nepal side. But this team, mostly from around Seattle, wanted to be the first Americans to climb Mt. Everest from the Tibet side. The first attempt came in 1982, but when team member Marty Hoey died on the mountain, the climb was called off. Now they were back.

Skip and I were members of the support team; I was the writer and Skip was the product supplier and friendly encourager to all. There was also a doctor and a videographer among us. We would spend a few days in each of the small villages along the way to base camp, in order to let our bodies and minds grow accustomed to the lack of oxygen in the ever-increasing altitudes of Tibet.

With each new adventure, Skip comes away with important lessons that can be applied to both life and business. In many ways, his experiences in the mountains and in nature have served as a kind of church for Skip, imparting wisdom to him and honing his legendary instincts. He has learned vividly that in order to achieve ones goals in the wilderness or on the mountain, one must be as perfectly prepared as possible and take the journey one step at a time. On these adventures and in business, Skip has learned to trust his instincts and to listen to the soft whispers that come from within. Sometimes listening closely to your inner self can save your life when high on a mountain determining a new route around the wreckage of a recent killer-avalanche, or your career when making business decisions.

However, personal growth doesn't have to always take place in exotic locales or during tough situations. People like Skip find adventure wherever they are. There is never a reason in life to be bored, no matter the circumstances.

Skip learned this important lesson early in life in the little town of Grainfield, Kansas (Population 291). The small community is surrounded by wheat fields as far as the eye can see. Even before Skip could walk, his mother would often have to go looking for him as he would crawl out of the house and head wherever his adventuresome heart called him to go. More often than not, he would be getting ready to crawl across the railroad tracks, or perhaps already had, on his way to the giant silver grain elevators. Maybe growing up in such a flat place and being attracted to those mountain-sized grain elevators is what planted the seed in Skip to be drawn to the tallest places on earth. Clearly, even as a toddler, he was never bored.

At the moment, Skip and I were fighting boredom in Tibet and were out for a walk in the tiny village. Being strangers in a strange land did not keep us inside. There were things to learn and adventures to be had. Although we didn't know one word of the local language, we were on a mission to find one of Skip's most favorite things in the world—beer. He was certain that even here, in one of the most spiritual places on earth, there must be beer somewhere.

As we walked through the dusty streets, we began to talk

xi

about how brilliant a leader Lou Whittaker was. Skip mentioned how it's absolutely essential to have the right team in order to achieve success in anything, a principle that can be applied to both mountain climbing and in business. Lou had certainly assembled a world-class team of mountaineers for the climb.

When deciding who to include on a team, whether it be for work or recreation, I have heard Skip say many times that it is based on what he or she delivers under extreme pressure while in the midst of the task. It has nothing to do with how prestigious their diploma is, how big their muscles are, or how bright their charismatic smile is. Skip had learned early on with the start of JanSport that success is all about performance and grace under pressure.

Surviving on the mountain and in the outdoor equipment business depends not only on having the right people, but also on having the right gear. Throughout their forty year history, Skip and JanSport have always believed in partnering with the right explorers. They also believe in relentlessly testing their equipment under the most extreme conditions in the world.

Years ago, Skip had given me the famous JanSport frame pack, the blue D-3, to walk across America with. The competing brand I started with fell apart before I got to New Orleans. I walked about three thousands miles with a D-3 on my back. In fact, I was the only person at that time to have ever worn through the pack's aluminum frame just from it constantly rubbing on my thigh. By building products tough enough to withstand the world's most demanding adventurers, Skip and JanSport knew that they could guarantee their products for the life of their 'normal' customers.

As for the little town we were exploring, there was nothing normal about it, at least to us. It would be dark in a few hours and we fell in behind the yak caravan on a single lane street filled with potholes. The Chinese Army trucks that we rode in on were about the only motorized vehicles anywhere to be found in the interior of Tibet.

A brightly colored, ancient wooden door opened ahead of us. From behind it walked a beautiful, black haired young woman. Some of the Tibetan women we had seen were exotic and attractive and innocently friendly. We were the first white men that many of them had ever seen. Surely Skip's light blond hair and my blue eyes were exotic looking to them. I suggested that maybe this twenty-something-year-old might be headed someplace where Skip could buy beer. We stopped following the yak caravan and discreetly began to follow her.

We followed her into a building that looked something like a school. For all we knew it could have been a bar or dance hall. The dark hallways led to an auditorium where there were close to a hundred people. We sat down and watched a black and white propaganda movie made by the Chinese conquerors of Tibet. Its plot trashed and vilified everything that was held dear by Tibetans and showed the Chinese riding in on white horses, literally, to save them. We left the movie without any beer but with the rarest of experiences, one that we would have never been introduced to by our Chinese guides.

Although we found no beer, we did find something far more memorable by following that beautiful young woman into that auditorium—the dark truth that mass media manipulation exists even out here in the holy mountains of the Tibetan people.

The next morning we continued our journey and soon found ourselves at base camp. Several weeks later our team became the first American team to summit Mt. Everest from the Tibet side, putting Phil Ershler on top of the world's tallest mountain.

This small story recounts only one among thousands of Skip's adventures. His adventuresome spirit symbolizes much about him and the way he has lived his life. He has trusted his instincts and taken huge risks. He has designed and manufactured fantastic outdoor products that have been tested by world-class adventurers whose lives often depend on this equipment. Through all of his experiences, he has maintained a positive and playful attitude which has helped to inspire many others along the way. Skip was never just about work, and he definitely was not in it for the money. Beer and fun always played a role.

Even during downtime, like our days hanging out in the hidden villages of Tibet, Skip found ways to have adventures, even if it began as a search for beer and ended up as something very different—something darkly inspiring and rare. When you begin to travel down a new road, you never know where you will end up. Sometimes you just follow where your gut tells you to go, enjoy the journey, and don't worry about the ending. Once that is over, go out and find another adventure. There's always another mountain to climb.

SOUNDTRACK SOLD SEPARATELY

I have a confession.

JanSport co-founders Murray Pletz, Jan Lewis, and I were not your typical business types. We were first and foremost hippies. But not hippies in the "Hollywood Stoner" version played by Cheech and Chong, or the likes of MTV's Pauly Shore who was most likely a product—literally—of the Sixties. We were a harmless bunch, preferring to tune in, turn on, and drop out of the expected societal norm. A walking stick and a daypack loaded with a few essentials enabled us to travel just about anywhere.

Like most hippies during the Summer of Love in '67, we were looking for a different path—and, to be sure, a road less traveled—thank you Robert Frost. The problem with roads, however, is that they are engineered, prescribed, scripted, and built for the masses. In our view, you could take the safe route and follow the highway or, ideally, blaze your own trail.

That's why at its core, JanSport is about the pursuit of freedom, individuality, and no boundaries. We've always appealed to the natural high that comes from getting outdoors and mixing it up with nature. Why is this important?

Ever since the question, "Why are we here?" burrowed its way into man's subconscious, there have been those who have made it their life's goal to discover all four corners of the Earth. I believe that one of our purposes in life is to absorb energies from all directions, thus becoming a whole, well-rounded person. How do you and I achieve this noble objective? Through adventure. For in the wandering lay many of life's secret joys.

In a way, JanSport was born to help fellow travelers walk to the beat of their own drummer. Cliché? To some. But this is the ideology that has enabled us to thrive since our humble beginnings in 1967. Founded on the principle of getting out and discovering life for yourself, JanSport has continuously broken down barriers in the "outdoor life" industry. We continue to do so today by making quality gear that is as fun as it is functional.

As you'll see, the history of JanSport plays out much like a movie script—a small, family business armed with a newfangled idea works out of a transmission shop and ultimately becomes one of the world's most recognized brands. We were confronted by reluctant lenders, skeptical customers, and a number of unlikely allies. And yet from this humble beginning, we managed to revolutionize the way the world plays outdoors and tackles the toughest mountains.

Candidly, the prospect of chronicling our great adventure was a daunting proposition. Being tied to a desk for long stretches of isolation and typing was almost as overwhelming as facing an avalanche on Mt. Rainier. I'd much rather feel the sun on my face than the constant flicker of an electromagnetic wave pattern emitted by a computer screen.

Nevertheless, I pressed on to write this book with the hope that you'll be inspired to break your routine, smash the mold, and chase a few of your own rainbows. Look, if three long-haired hippies with little more to their names than a thirst for high adventure and a love for the outdoors can change history and be successful in business, so can you!

By the time you reach the last page, you'll know who we were, what we did, and why it mattered. You'll meet some very special friends who enriched our lives and helped us climb a few mountains along the way. And, I trust, you'll discover that the rich pool of inspiration and creativity necessary to succeed in business awaits you if you make time to occasionally escape from the concrete jungle.

Although I've worked hard to retell the JanSport story, the telling wouldn't be complete without the music. So many of our experiences and adventures were accompanied by the soundtrack of the Sixties. The fresh, fun, melodic, and emotionally-charged music of that era was an invitation to grab the nearest magic carpet and ride, captain, ride, into a groovy kind of love, complete with flowers in our hair. That being said, this story is best *experienced* when read with a classic rock station or old Dylan album playing in the background.

So, if you're ready, let's hit the dusty trail.

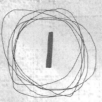

BORN TO BE WILD

I have a theory that goes something like this: the feisty, freedom-loving spirit of JanSport is a direct byproduct of the Wild West.

You see, at the time of my birth, my parents were living in Grainfield, Kansas. Since the town's population was just under 100, there was no hospital. My folks had to drive seventy miles over the flat and dusty Kansas prairie to the nearest hospital in Hays.

It's the dust that I want you to focus on.

About a hundred years before I was born, Wild Bill Hickok—the legendary western gunslinger and gambler—was serving as the Sheriff and Marshal of Hays. Left-handed yet always quick on the draw, Wild Bill was downright handy with a rifle or knife. He routinely rounded up notorious renegades and rabble-rousers. Credited as the person who invented the idea of "posting" warnings to outlaws on the Dead Man's Tree, Hickok would put criminals on notice: either get out of town by sundown or be shot on sight the next day.

Few lingered to find out if he meant business.

This might explain why Wild Bill, born James Butler Hickok, became the hero of the first American dime novel. Tales of his gutsy adventures spread far and wide. Like a hippie forerunner, Wild Bill sported a handlebar mustache and long, shoulder-length hair. While he was shooting bad guys, drinking beer, and winning at cards, another Wild West legend was afoot, kicking up the Kansas dust.

Frontiersman William Frederick Cody, better known as Buffalo Bill, was hired to scout Indians and shoot buffalo for the Kansas Pacific Railroad as they laid tracks through Kansas towards Denver. For several years, Hays was also home to this colorful character. Although known to be a rough and tough outdoorsman, Buffalo Bill was a showman at heart. Eventually his traveling Wild West show became world famous.

Not too far off, General George Custer was stationed at Fort Riley, Kansas where he was assigned to the 7th U.S. Cavalry. He also had a brief stint kicking up dust and barking orders at Fort Hays, Kansas.

Back to my theory.

I believe the fighting spirit of these men must have lingered in the dust of Hays, Kansas. Like a well-preserved fossil, wisps of their DNA must have been trapped in the hard Kansas soil. After all, Hays is well-known for the fossils that are buried in its windswept prairies. Somehow a fragment of General Custer, Wild Bill, and Buffalo Bill's rowdy thirst for adventure found its way into my bloodstream. Don't ask me how—there are many things medical science can't explain.

As you'll see in the pages ahead, I've always gravitated toward a freedom-loving, trail-blazing lifestyle on par with these rough-hewn frontiersmen. So has JanSport. A coincidence? Maybe...but maybe not.

Granted, some would point to the bloodstock of my own family tree. My grandfather, Charlie Yowell, was both a genuine cowboy and a skilled rancher who staked his claim in Western Kansas. He was a hard-drinking, backcountry maverick who had a real love of the outdoors and an unmatched knack for trading mules, cattle, and horses. On my mother's side and heralding from Seattle, Washington, there was my grandfather, Captain John Murray. My cousin Murray Pletz, co-founder of JanSport, got his name and zany, impulsive drive from him.

During the Gold Rush of the 1890s, Captain Murray was the youngest pilot of a Sternwheeler (a steamboat propelled by a large paddle wheel) which shuttled miners from Seattle to Skagway, Alaska and back until 1933. A fearless young man who never met a challenge too tough, friends gave him the nickname "Kid Captain of the Yukon," since he was the first to navigate the uncharted Five-Finger Rapids of the Yukon River.

While living in Alaska, he also befriended two prolific writers: the acclaimed Jack London, author of more than fifty books, and Robert W. Service, who penned nineteen works, a number of which chronicled tales from the Gold Rush. Not only did my grandfather have a life of adventure, he hung out with a couple of storytellers who were always quick to spin a tall tale or two.

Whether my deep affinity for the untamed wilderness was passed down from my grandparents or from some connection to Custer, Wild Bill, and Buffalo Bill, I can't say for sure. At the very least, the legacy they left in dusty pages of American history made a lasting impression on my spirit. What is certain is that my parents played a significant role in setting the stage for the man I was to become. Come to think of it, my dad, Harold "Spoof" Yowell, had his share of unconventional pursuits, not the least of which was a Donkey Polo competition I'll explain later on.

MAMAS AND THE PAPAS

As I was preparing to work on this book, I rummaged through several boxes of photographs and stumbled on one taken during my early childhood in Grainfield, Kansas. Back then my parents were poor. Not dirt poor, but close. In spite of our tight finances, I had a look of sheer joy and total contentment on my face. My mother, Marjorie, had placed me in an old, galvanized washtub for a bath. A white, single-story home with clapboard siding was in the background, complete with a clothesline stretched from the back door to some unseen point in the yard.

We had an outhouse several steps behind our bungalow with one bedroom, a kitchen, and a small living room. Without plumbing, we used a hand pump in the backyard for water. The fact that my folks owned a home so soon after the Great Depression was pretty phenomenal. While the house is no longer there, and an assortment of weeds cover the empty lot where the house once

1946: Skip bathing in Grainfield, Kansas

stood, I have some great memories from that time. I cherish the love and care I received from the hands of my parents.

Dad was born and raised with the small-town family values that life in Grainfield provided. As one of *fifteen* kids, money was scarce. Dad delivered milk before school, raised a skinny chicken to health and sold it for a buck, and later on, was hired by the local baseball teams as a freelance pitcher. The teams paid him with fresh produce, food, and sometimes money. He was so good in sports that he was awarded a partial college scholarship and even played a little Minor League baseball.

But with the attack on Pearl Harbor in December of 1941, America was drawn into World War II. Dad promptly enlisted in the U.S. Army and served until 1945. About the same time that he was getting out of the armed forces, my mother was visiting a friend in Chicago.

Mom was a Seattle girl who lived on scenic Green Lake just north of town. She worked in a bank and, during the war, took a second job at Boeing. She was married briefly to a tank commander

9

Mom and Dad in Chicago.

who was stationed in Europe during World War II. Sadly, he was killed just six months after their wedding.

Always a sharp dresser down to the fur coat, mom's winsome smile and good looks caught my father's eye as he passed through Chicago. They met, fell in love, and made immediate plans to marry. I tend to think that my dad might have done some serious sweet talking to convince a big city girl to move to Grainfield, Kansas.

The first order of business was to travel together by train to Fort Sill, Oklahoma where Dad would be discharged from the Army. Then Dad thought it would be a good idea to make a detour south and exchange vows on the steps of the Alamo in San Antonio, Texas—a place where Texans fought and died to preserve their freedom during the Texas Revolution of 1863. I'd say that fits neatly into my theory about my being linked to the Wild West. (Keep in mind that famed frontiersman Davy Crockett died in that battle.) Perhaps a bit of Davy's genetic code clung to my mom's skirt when Dad swept her off her feet and carried her across the Alamo threshold.

Stranger things have happened.

Having successfully tied the knot, my parents made their way to Grainfield to settle down. In each town or city where they stopped along the way from Texas to Kansas, my mother would ask, "Honey, is Grainfield as big as this town?"

Dad would smile and say, "No, not quite." Of course, Dad must have known that Grainfield—with just one main street and no stop lights—was sure to be a bit of a shock.

When they arrived and Mom got her first look at her new home, she cried. In fact, she cried every night for a few weeks. Grainfield wasn't even close to the size of Seattle. I imagine Dad tried his level best to put a proper spin on things. He might have pointed to the Grainfield Opera House, the only two-story structure in town, and described its grand history. After all, it was home to various vaudeville shows, comedians, and jazz bands.

It wasn't long before mom came to accept her new life and surroundings. She discovered she enjoyed hunting for arrowheads and other Native American artifacts. That was one of those interests she passed on to me. And, being a former Seattle socialite, mom started a club called the "Do What You Want to Do" club. She pulled together a group of local ladies who met once a week and did whatever they wanted to do. With a spunky attitude like that, I'd say mom had been touched by the spirit of the Wild West for sure.

DONKEY POLO

I was born in 1946. With my arrival, dad had to find creative ways to pay the bills. Dad's first job out of the Army was working at Shaw Motor Company where he held an entry level position that didn't pay much. That's when his entrepreneurial spirit kicked into high gear. In addition to the weekly dances he promoted at the Opera House, he decided to sponsor a regular Donkey Polo match— a hilarious parody of the traditional polo match. Opponents would swing brooms rather than mallets to knock around plastic balls instead of a wooden polo ball. Rather than ride horses, team members mounted donkeys . . . which, trust me, aren't as cooperative as their horse cousins.

Dad scraped together the money to purchase ten donkeys from eastern Colorado—a pricey purchase because meat was scarce due to the war. He engaged teams from two adjacent communities to play each other in a field at the edge of town. He printed up handbills to promote the competitions, and the locals paid a modest ticket price to attend. Many placed bets on their favorite team on the side.

Dad's creative, inventive, and "can do" spirit made a lasting impression on me. I watched him dream, make a plan, execute his plan, and, in the end, saw that a good time was had by all. Although I imagine my mom might have wondered on more than one occasion what her classy friends back in Seattle would have thought if they ever caught her at a Donkey Polo match.

While these contests were a big hit, one of the donkeys was responsible for my first scar. Just for a lark, my folks decided to put me on a donkey and take a picture when I was about three years old. Unfortunately, the beast was acting cantankerous either from having played a hard game of polo or just because he was a jackass. Whatever the reason, he threw me into a barbwire fence and gashed my right kneecap.

Thankfully, that little accident didn't prevent Mom and Dad from encouraging me to push the limits, to try new things, to hunt, fish, hike, water ski, and explore my world. For example, at a young

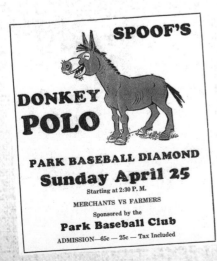

SPOOF'S

DONKEY POLO

PARK BASEBALL DIAMOND

Sunday April 25

Starting at 2:30 P.M.

MERCHANTS VS FARMERS

Sponsored by the

Park Baseball Club

ADMISSION—65c — 25c — Tax Included

age and at the encouragement of my mom, a friend and I hiked out to a small stream in the woods. It was a good two or three mile trek out in the country from our house. That was my first use of a pack. I used my dad's army pack. With Mom's help, we filled a canteen with juice and stuffed sandwiches and snacks into that rucksack.

I didn't realize it at the time, but later on I could see how my parents' belief in me gave me confidence. They imparted to me a picture of the amazing things that existed outside of my small world. Because my mom grew up in Seattle, she constantly drew upon her big-city knowledge to expand my horizons beyond the flat, sandy soil of Grainfield.

For his part, there wasn't a lazy bone in Dad's body. He often had to work three jobs to pay our bills. Ultimately, Dad tried his hand in the oil business. Our family moved to Russell, Kansas, the birthplace of Senator Bob Dole. Dad worked his way up the ladder from a roughneck to a "pump-around"—which is a person who checks the tank levels to see how full they were of oil.

After a season of hard work and learning the ropes, we moved again to Great Bend, Kansas. Dad took a job with the Kaiser-Francis oil company, the largest independent oil company in the country then, and in time, owned his own gas station for extra income. No question, those hard times instilled a strict work ethic in my dad, and he passed it on to me.

At his encouragement, I worked a part-time job in the oil fields. You could make a lot of money back in those days as a young kid if you didn't mind laboring in the oil field under filthy, hard, semi-dangerous conditions. A lot of guys I worked with had fingers missing.

I'll never forget one day as we were pulling rods on an oil well when the rod came back and hit me in the head. Thankfully, I was wearing a hard hat which suffered a giant dent. One of my co-workers said, "Skip, I want you to put that helmet on your desk when you get back to school. That will be your motivation to continue in your studies." You might say that experience stuck in my mind.

13

My parents always wanted me to go to college, something neither one of them completed. Indeed, after the close call in the oil field, lifting books in college instead of oil rods was looking pretty good to me. In 1964, I attended Wichita State University for a year with an eye on playing baseball and entering the Air Force ROTC program. You see, I had this crazy desire to learn to fly a plane.

That's when I was thrown a serious curveball.

None of us anticipated the fact that in 1967 I'd get a phone call from my cousin Murray—one that would change the course of history not just for me, but for how the entire world would come to enjoy the great outdoors.

While I'll save that story for the next chapter, there is one last coincidence I must point out. The movie *Butch Cassidy and the Sundance Kid* was released in 1969 during the early days of JanSport, and it was based upon the life of the legendary train and bank robbers. Butch Cassidy's exploits included robbing trains on—get this—the Union Pacific Railroad.

Do you see the implication here?

Allow me to connect the dots back to my theory.

Buffalo Bill was employed by the Union Pacific Railroad . . . Butch Cassidy robbed trains that ran on those rails. Who knows whether or not a fragment of Butch Cassidy's DNA found its way to Hays? It could have happened. The film was even released precisely as we were launching JanSport, which could explain why Murray and I watched the movie every night for at least two weeks in a row. We must have been cosmically connected to that bit of Wild West history.

At least that's my opinion, and I'm sticking with it.

EARLY DAZE

*I*f you had told me in 1967 that JanSport would one day celebrate forty years of innovation, adventure, and general outdoor grooviness, I might have said you were either pulling my leg or high on something. But we defied the odds and the host of naysayers who thought we couldn't succeed in business without wingtips and pressed pants. What started out as my cousin Murray's pipe dream, evolved into an international company selling several million packs a year.

Sorta makes me wonder what was in Murray's pipe.

Whether produced by an underground psycho-active substance, or inspired by the peace, love, and flower power vibe that filled the air, having a vision in the Sixties wasn't all that uncommon. So when Murray said that he had a vision of building better frame packs and selling them to climbers, I wasn't shocked. Everybody was having visions and mystical experiences.

Remembering them—well, that was something else entirely.

Thankfully, I had the foresight to carry my camera with me to capture—and thereby remember—the action. You see, ever since I was a teenager, I wanted to study photography. I had even made plans to attend the Brooks Institute of Photography. However, as Mick Jagger and the Rolling Stones who had their share of visions sang, "You can't always get what you want / but if you try sometimes you just might find you get what you need." Right on, brother.

Before I took my shot at pursuing photography, Murray made me an offer I couldn't refuse. Okay, I could have turned him down, but since he and I shared so many great outdoor adventures during our childhood, it just made sense to go with the flow.

I remember in junior high school I spent several summers in Seattle with Murray and the Pletz family. It was then that I learned how amazingly skilled my Uncle Norman was in the field of engineering.

During the 1950s as a hobby, Uncle Norm was part of a pit crew for one of the hydroplane boats used in the annual race held on Lake Washington each summer. For fun, Uncle Norm built several small hydroplane boats of his own. His family and I used them to explore a beautiful small lake near the Canadian border that summer. We had the coolest time fishing, hiking, and staying in a cottage cabin on the lake with bonfires every night. These visits allowed Murray and me to bond on a number of fronts: outdoors, music, antiques, and exploring the back roads of Eastern Washington.

With that shared history, how could I turn him down?

Besides, it was clear that Murray had inherited a creative gene from his dad, Uncle Norm. After high school, Murray went on to major in Industrial Design at the University of Washington. One of his projects was to make something unique out of aluminum. Drawing upon his years of experience and his knowledge of hiking, Murray invented an adjustable aluminum frame for backpacking—one that allowed for individual precision fitting. Thanks to the aluminum, his frame was both lightweight and very strong. It was much more versatile than the welded frame which had been the standard for years. Because of his design, he won an award for best use of aluminum from the Alcoa Company.

Probably the smartest thing Murray did was to immediately get a patent on the construction of that frame. The next smartest thing was when he offered to name his company after his girlfriend, Jan Peterson. While they were dating, Jan received a teaching degree from the University of Washington. She also was very talented on her home sewing machine working with fabric and patterns.

In 1967, Murray said, "Jan, if you marry me, I'll name the company after you." She did, and he did, and JanSport was born. He had the frame patent and she had the skill with fabric. It was a marriage made in frame pack heaven.

17

Now that Murray and Jan had the foundation for their fledgling endeavor, they needed someone to convince stores to buy their product. That's when I got the call from Murray asking me to join the business and handle the sales and marketing. I did, and my life has been forever changed.

(L to R) Jan, Skip, and Murray for a catalog cover. Photo by Marsha Burns.

Like I said at the outset, I would *never* have predicted that we three hippies would revolutionalize an industry. We were the new kids on the block. There was no business plan. We had no special training. We had even less money. We didn't even have a store. All we had was Murray's innovative design, Jan's skill, my creative instincts and love of people, and a shared affinity for Dylan music and beer. That was enough for me.

My decision wasn't as crazy as it might sound on the surface. I knew that the Pacific Northwest had a rich heritage of being an outdoor and mountaineering community. For example, *The Mountaineers* was an outdoor club that had been training people in mountaineering skills for 70 years. And there were several successful outdoor gear companies such as Eddie Bauer and REI who had found a way to be profitable.

What's more, we learned that there were no pack manufacturers located in the Pacific Northwest. The Kelty company was making welded frames in California while CampTrails was making welded packs in Arizona. Nobody had a flexible frame— because Murray had just invented it. And, with the absence of manufactures in the heart of the outdoor country, my gut told me we had an opportunity to make our mark with this new product. I abandoned my dreams of photography and relocated to Seattle to pursue Murray's vision.

SHIFTING INTO HIGH GEAR

My Uncle Norm owned a transmission repair shop on the corner of 175th and Aurora Avenue in North Seattle. The two-story building, about three double garages in size, was nestled against a hill. His workshop occupied the lower ground floor. Upstairs at street level was a large, open, and unused room. Wanting to give us our first break, Norm invited us to rent the empty space.

There was one problem. While there would be heat, he explained, there wasn't any air conditioning. Still, we liked the location for two reasons. First, it was directly across the street from the famous Parker's Ballroom, home to many hot local and touring bands. We pictured wandering over after work for live music and brew. Secondly, next door was a cool motorcycle shop. Since one of Murray's passions was racing motocross, this was definitely an added bonus. What the dusty room may have lacked in the way of creature comforts was more than compensated for by its proximity to the things we liked. We took the space.

From 1967 to 1971, it served as the headquarters for JanSport—not to mention it was also where I slept for a while. Like I said, we had very little money. While Murray and Jan lived at her parents' home, I had a fold-up cot in the back of the JanSport "factory." In the morning, I'd make a pot of coffee for breakfast. We worked hard all day, hand-making every aspect of our packs. Lunch was a luxury. For dinner, we'd get a giant block of cheese, maybe some crackers, several bottles of the cheapest beer we could afford, listen to Dylan music, and play guitars until the wee hours.

Before long, we filled up the workspace with hard, wooden benches for making the frames, sewing machines, boxes of supplies and raw materials, assorted bending tools, and bolts of fabric. We saved a little spot near my cot for the finished bags. To say we lived and breathed JanSport 24/7 would be accurate. Even the weekends were spoken for. We'd go hiking with our gear,

19

Skip and Gombu the dog backpacking.
Photo by Bruce Wade.

both for fun and to test its functionality and durability. While on the trail, we'd meet other hiker-types and engage in product talk. By Monday morning, we'd regroup at the factory to discuss what needed to be changed or improved.

From the start, JanSport was a family affair. My Aunt Mabel, Norm's wife, handled the bookkeeping. Jan, who owned her own sewing machine, taught my sister Diana how to sew. Murray's brother Ken and my brother Randy pitched in during the summer months with the assembly process. And Uncle Norm and my dad designed the necessary bending equipment because we couldn't just go out and buy what we needed to make our frame.

At first we used hand-benders to shape the aluminum tubing into pack frames. Later on we progressed to a hydraulic system we designed using hydraulics purchased from the Boeing surplus office across town.

Both my father and Uncle Norm lived through the depression era when money and resources were scarce. People didn't just throw everything away like they do today. They understood what it meant to make magic—that is, to take something that had been used, recycle it, and, in our case, turn it into a key tool for a low price.

I learned from Uncle Norm and my father's creativity and frugal example how to be resourceful, especially when resources weren't plentiful. Given the reality that virtually *everything* we did in the beginning was breaking new ground and that we experienced more famine than feast, that was a much needed lesson. Let me tell you, we had to harness every ounce of our creative juices to fuel the operation. What's amazing is that we didn't kill each other in the process. In fact, quite the opposite happened.

If we hit an obstacle, we worked around it. If one person was having a bad day, we pulled together, supported him or her, and got through it as a team. Just as we had to rely on one another when climbing, we looked out for each other in the shop. What's more, regardless of the pressures we faced or the blur of activity that defined our days, we were determined to have a good time doing it.

FOUR GUIDING PRINCIPLES

I'm often asked about what made those early days so special. People always want to know about our defining principles or our core pillars of belief that sustained our success. That has always been difficult for me to answer, primarily because Murray, Jan, and I never sat down to formalize a company position. We never had that kind of time. Besides, if there had been a few extra unclaimed minutes in the day, we'd much rather cruise across the street to see who was playing at Parker's Ballroom.

But now that I'm in a reflective mood, I'd say that there have been four principles we instinctively embraced. I'd also say that they have served us well for four decades and will continue to do so until everyone on the planet catches the good vibrations and owns a JanSport pack.

We'll succeed because we will work the hardest
We value and appreciate each person
We believe there's more to life than a day's work
We'll make fun a part of everything we do

Going a step further, the essence of JanSport is about the spirit of freedom. It's the feeling that comes when we get outdoors to smell the fresh air and let the mountains speak to us. JanSport has always been about tapping into the absolute fun that's in each of us—no matter what our age. We love bringing out the kid-like playfulness, discovery, and awe that draws young and old alike outside to have fun and seek adventure.

To this day, that's what employees love about JanSport. If you were to talk to anybody that has ever been involved with the company, they'll tell you we work hard, but we still maintain that big, "happy family" feel where each person is valued. What else would you expect from a hippie who refuses to wear wingtips?

AIN'T NO MOUNTAIN HIGH ENOUGH

*I*n the early days of JanSport, we were pioneers. We had no map to follow, no mentor to consult, and no memory of what worked before because there was no before. We were just making it up as we went along. Everything we attempted to do was new and untested because the outdoor industry was an emerging industry. In many cases, we set the pace through trial and error and everybody else followed.

Those early days were exhilarating and frustrating, energizing and draining, all at the same time. Just when we thought we had a breakthrough, a fresh set of roadblocks or challenges would surface. Like a game of whack-a-mole, we'd knock down one problem and another one poked up his ugly head in a different spot: cash shortages, bank credit-line hassles, fire damage, legal minefields, theft, machine failure, bad beer.

And yet, convinced that we had a winner with Murray's patented design, we pressed on to blaze our trail and make our mark. After all, a pioneer is focused, committed, and convinced that the effort, the isolation, and the hard times will be worth the payoff—one day. We knew the whole venture could flop. Then again, we thought there might just be gold in 'dem 'dar hills. Murray, Jan, and I would never know until we staked our claim and dug in for all we were worth.

For three hippies going into business, I think being naïve had its advantages. We were young, energetic, and maintained a "we can conquer anything" mindset. Not knowing the full picture was a benefit to us because we couldn't pre-judge the outcome. We didn't put boundaries on anything we tried. If we could dream it, we tried it. Either it worked or it didn't. Indeed, having an open mind and a determined spirit empowered us to think out of the box to try different things without a fear of failure. For us, ignorance was bliss.

By 1970, we got into a real groove manufacturing packs in the factory above my uncle's transmission shop. We poured our hearts and souls into getting every last stitch perfect. We were in control of every aspect of the production and assembly process and had nobody else to blame if things weren't right. Nothing was farmed

Tent ad from the 1970s by Heckler-Bowker

out in those early days. We bent the frames, cut the fabric from hand-drawn patterns, and sewed the zippers into place. Like proud parents fawning over a newborn, we paid attention to the smallest detail.

It was also deeply important to us that every JanSport pack we put out there was the best in function, quality, and value for the money. Period. The last thing we wanted to do was sell a product just to make a buck on it. If we had to climb a few mountains—either a mountain of problems in the business world, or Mt. Rainier—then so be it. We had our eye on being number one.

FROM BABIES TO BEST SELLERS

Creating a great product is one thing. Convincing others to buy your goods is the real challenge—at least until you gain a solid reputation. The sales job fell on my shoulders, a task made difficult because of the ongoing state of chaos in the office. Since space was at a premium, we were constantly bumping into one another or stepping around stacks of supplies or finished products. The noise level, while not unbearable, was constant; the drone of sewing machines was punctuated by the grunts and groans of someone bending a frame by hand.

Now that Jan was a new mom, she would come to work carrying her baby Heidi in a basket. Staying home was not an option since we needed Jan's sewing skills. The safest spot in the factory was adjacent to my desk, so Jan often plopped Heidi's carrier next to my workspace. Heidi was as adorable as the next baby, but just imagine making a sales call accompanied by the incessant wails of a tired newborn.

In spite of the general bedlam, I managed to land a few big fish. Things were beginning to look up. Our largest single sale at that point had been an order of twenty-five scout packs for Recreational Equipment, Inc. (REI) right before the Fourth of July.

If REI's order of twenty-five units was a big fish, I would soon land a few whales. I remember walking into the factory waving a sales order above my head as I announced our largest order: 300 packs for Eddie Bauer. That was the day JanSport was changed forever. We were no longer a mom and pop operation. With that sale, we had blazed a path into the big leagues and were now a serious manufacturing player.

What does any business worth its salt do when it comes to a crossroad? They call a meeting. I decided the time had come for us to have a serious pow wow. We needed to figure out how we'd handle this massive order.

You could feel the excitement as our little team gathered around the cutting table to formulate a plan. We knew this order had to be fulfilled as efficiently as was possible but with our JanSport quality. Each of us knew this was our big chance to showcase our commitment to excellence. Sloppiness wouldn't be tolerated and quality would never be sacrificed.

I explained that Eddie Bauer wanted us to build four different frame packs for use in their retail outlets and in their mail order catalog. There were so many specifics to get the production underway. The design work would be done by Murray. Jan would make the patterns. We needed the special Eddie Bauer green fabric, labels, and a host of other raw materials. Each pack had to be individually boxed, too.

Having an extra set of hands to make the pack frames was

essential. I called and hired Paul Folds, a childhood friend from back in Kansas. Paul came and got more out of the deal than he ever expected. While working at JanSport, he met his future wife at Parker's Ballroom across the street and was married in a wedding chapel on Aurora Avenue around the corner. Not a bad deal if you ask me.

In addition to his extra help, we needed a credit line at the bank to purchase certain supplies. This was a massive hurdle. Remember, we were pioneering new turf. Nobody in the financial services world wanted to go out on a limb. Once again, Uncle Norman came to the rescue. This time he offered to personally guarantee the loan.

We were especially fortunate when a number of our key suppliers agreed to provide us with credit, including YKK, Waterbury Buckle, Travis, Howe & Bainbridge, and Alcoa.

With everything in place, we got busy.

SIGNED, SEALED, AND DELIVERED

After production of the packs was completed, we loaded up the delivery van. She was an old, blue Dodge with the spare tire mounted on the front engine grill like some sort of rubberized cattle prod. Uncle Norm had worked on the van's transmission for a customer who, in turn, had plans to sell it. Even with the high mileage—something in excess of 100,000—and the fact that it burned oil and had very little power, the price was right so we bought it. Almost overnight, the Blue Van became a regular member of the JanSport family.

Because the back of the van was an empty shell, we could stuff in 106 individually boxed packs to take to the Eddie Bauer warehouse. My heart raced a little as I went to deliver the first load to the warehouse. This was a big deal for us. I was proud of the hard

work the team exhibited, the way we managed to maintain our high standard of quality and, thankfully, the chance to pick up a check for the work.

In addition to hauling boxes, we'd take the Blue Van on weekend climbing trips to the Northwest. Once, Keith Roush and I were on a weekend adventure when the Blue Van overheated. Since there was no place to get water for miles, we solved the problem by pouring beer in

1970s Yukon tent ad. Photo by Marsha Burns.

the radiator. Let's just say that pioneers are known for their creative solutions. In hindsight, I wonder if the Blue Van could have been cited for drinking and driving.

Speaking of creative ideas, one day Murray, feeling inspired by some unseen vision, grabbed a blow torch and cut off the front portion of the van's roof. Removing the panel just above the front two seats, he affixed snaps around the new roof opening and Jan made a snap-off sunroof out of pack cloth. It wasn't pretty, but it sure was fun.

I don't want to give you the impression that we were the only company with new ideas in those days. At the time we were pioneering packs, the DuPont company was searching for a tough new nylon to be used as a tire yarn. When what they created didn't work out for use in tires, they turned the nylon into a woven fabric. We bought the first bolt of that fabric and used it in our prototype daypacks. It was lightweight yet durable, rugged, and could take a lot of abuse. DuPont called it Cordura which turned out to be our biggest breakthrough in raw material. Plus, it made a cool sunroof for the van.

We were using traditional metal zippers on our packs made by Coats & Clark when Mike Stroud, a representative from the YKK company, called on us to demonstrate their new nylon coil zippers. We loved their improved design because they didn't freeze up like the metal zippers in cold temperatures and were much easier to zip. We rapidly changed over to YKK's all nylon coils. That refinement was another breakthrough feature which we still use today.

Before long, JanSport outgrew the transmission shop. We didn't have enough capital to relocate to larger quarters—at least not yet. A creative, no-cost solution was needed. We decided to outsource production by enlisting a number of home sewers in Winthrop which was way across the northern Cascades. Talented people would come by and pick up a box of parts and then take them home to sew and assemble the items into finished bags. We also enlisted the help of another company, Roffe Skiwear. During their off-season, we sent parts and raw materials to Roffe who would make bags for us in their shop.

As our sales continued to soar, the need for a more permanent space became painfully evident, so we moved from the transmission shop in north Seattle to Paine Field in Everett, Washington. Our new location was an old, renovated army barracks building that cost just three cents a square foot to rent. We had a much bigger building than we were used to and we were able to increase our capacity to thirty sewing machine operators. Eventually, we had to rent another barracks unit, the mess hall, and the chapel just to fit in our entire operation. We remained on-site there up until the early 1990s.

From that humble beginning in Uncle Norman's transmission shop, we filled three separate factories in Wenatchee, Washington and in Bayview, Washington during the 1980s. Today, we have operations in several countries around the world and employ more than four hundred people.

I'm sometimes asked whether or not a JanSport-type upstart company could be successfully launched in today's business environment. You know, if other twenty-something kids with a big idea were to drop out of college, could they pull it off? I'd offer a qualified yes. The key is whether or not they have the true spirit of a pioneer, one that is focused, committed, and convinced that their efforts and the hard times will be worth the payoff.

If you need proof, just look at Google, Ben & Jerry's, Starbucks and Papa John's.

Just remember, for the pioneer, life is an adventure and the path is unknown. But for those with a passion for their dreams, no mountain is too high.

Phrusumba, Murray, Jan, Skip, and Gombu for a catalog cover. Photo by Marsha Burns.

PACK MENTALITY

When Murray, Jan and I launched JanSport, we were labeled a lot of things—many were not exactly praiseworthy. My favorite wisecrack was that the three of us were "nothing more than a bunch of long-haired hippies who spent too much time above the tree line." I stand guilty as charged. We *did* have long hair. But as Larry Norman a musician and fellow long-hair sang back then, "They say to cut my hair / they're driving me insane / I grew it out long / to make room for my brain."

As for living life north of the tree line, there's no question that we were adrenaline junkies with a passion for adventure. In my view, the additional brain space afforded by our long hair and those frequent outdoor treks produced a host of cool product ideas for JanSport. Come to think of it, I'd bet my last Peter Max cosmic poster that our floral bell bottoms somehow played a part in our idea formation process. (I've also heard that a pizza with anchovies and double mushrooms can provide a wealth of inspiration—but that's another matter.)

Looking back, most of our product ideas came from two sources: 1) listening to others, and 2) real life, hands-on experiences in the wilderness. Out on the trail we'd meet other climbers, hikers, and wilderness enthusiasts who'd say, "Gee, Skip, wouldn't it be great to have an extra pocket?" or, "A zipper that doesn't freeze up would be cool," or, "I'd love it if there was a place to hang my ice axe off of the pack."

After hiking, we would return to the shop and use those new ideas to make our gear even more functional. Admittedly, when it comes to taking a new idea and developing it into a workable product, there's a big difference between *theory* and *practice*. For instance, when designing something for the outdoors, we had to factor in unpredictable and often severe weather conditions. As much as we might have been tempted to say, *Well, I know this idea will work because mechanically it should*, we knew that nothing could replace actual testing in the field.

We personally used *everything* we made. Not only did we test our product ideas thoroughly, we invited many of our climbing friends to do testing for us as well. As a result, when a JanSport

product came to the market for consumers, we knew it was going to work for them. And,

Jan and Skip with the Captain America framepack and the K2 barn in the background. Photo by Murray Pletz.

even though we were peace-loving hippies, we gladly put our products through hell to test their strength and reliability. That way we could place our lifetime warranty on them with confidence.

Clearly, one of the keys to our on-going success is that we are unafraid of identifying, pursuing, and testing new ideas. Not all ideas will work, of course. Some ideas are innovative, but lack mass appeal and are not profitable. Other ideas appear great on the surface, but flop after testing. And let's not forget that there are also the downright harebrained ideas. Case in point.

ACAPULCO OR BUST

I've always had a willingness to embrace a new idea and ride it for all it was worth—no matter how far-fetched it appeared at first. During the pre-JanSport days of the summer of 1966, I was working at a job in Estes Park, Colorado. Towards the end of summer, three friends from Kansas drove West to hang out with me.

With the fall semester of college rapidly approaching and my work in Estes Park finished, we got this off-the-wall idea to go to Mexico. In fact, we wanted to go all the way to the ocean and decided that Acapulco would be a cool spot to check out. We had no idea Acapulco was several thousand miles away. And we didn't know that you couldn't just drive across the border into Mexico without a visa. However, I'm not sure knowing those details would have changed our minds anyway.

With our sights set on a good time south of the border, Dannis Robison, Rick Douglas, Karl Moffett, and I hopped into Karl's 1962 black Chevy Impala and hit the road. Riding with us was my dog, *Socrates*, a beagle. One of the guys had a credit card. The rest of

33

us had a small amount of cash. But Acapulco was calling, and we weren't about to let the lack of funds keep us from heeding the call.

That's when we had another brainstorm. To save money, we decided we could sleep in jails instead of motel rooms. We targeted little towns along the way, and upon arrival, we would track down the magistrate and give him our hard-luck story . . . that we needed to conserve resources . . . that we were going back to college and didn't have a lot of extra money . . . that the four of us couldn't sleep in the car with a dog.

They agreed virtually every time. Depending on the jail, the police would either lock us up in a cell, or they'd shut us in the station and lock the front door. Like I said, these were Andy of Mayberry-sized jails without real inmates behind bars. Dannis wasn't crazy about the idea of being totally locked up so he decided to sleep in the back seat of the car. The rest of us slept in three or four jails on the way down to El Paso.

Of course, then there was the issue of food. By the time we reached Cimarron, New Mexico, money was really tight. That's when we discovered the Philmont Scout Ranch, the famous Boy Scout camping facility that sat on 127,395 gorgeous acres. Hungry for anything to eat at this point, we approached the mess hall and asked if we could have any food they might be planning to toss. To our pleasant surprise, they loaded us up with extra bologna, butter sandwiches, and frozen doughnuts.

Thankful for the freebies, we pressed on. We reached El Paso and crossed the border heading south toward the Mexican town of Juarez. We rode for maybe ten miles when we stumbled upon a lone government outpost staffed by the Mexican border patrol. A guard standing in the middle of the street signaled for us to stop. Karl lowered the music and rolled down the window.

The guard approached, circled the car, and peered inside. He said, "Do you have visas? Are you over 21?"

Visa? This was news to us. With a jab of his finger to the north, he told us that we'd have to go back to the American Consulate to get visas. To make matters worse, he confiscated Socrates and intended to keep him quarantined for thirty days.

We turned around and went to the American Consulate thinking we could get visas on the spot, only to be informed we had to have our parents' permission to get visas since we were all under twenty-one. Our parents didn't even know where we were, and calling them was not a pleasant option. Just like that, our dreams of sipping Coronas on the beach evaporated. However, we couldn't just leave—Socrates was still locked up!

As the afternoon drifted into evening, one of the guys snuck across the border into the area where Socrates was being held, got him out—don't ask me how—and brought him back. We quickly hid him in the back seat of the car and covered him with a blanket. Thankfully, we headed back to Estes Park without further hassles. Several days later, we were back in Colorado.

After returning from the short-lived vacation, Both Karl and Rick got a job at the Molybdenum mine in Cripple Creek and planned to stay in Colorado. Meanwhile, Dannis and I still needed to get back to Kansas to start college—without money and without a car. We had no choice but to hitchhike with my dog. A friend dropped us off on I-70 and, with thumbs extended, we started hitchhiking back to Kansas.

Fortunately, we were traveling light. I had a duffle bag and

35

Dannis had his stuff in a Kotex box—an odd choice, I know. Needing something to carry his things in, we stopped by a grocery store and asked for a box. It wasn't until we were out on the freeway that we realized that Dannis was a walking billboard for feminine hygiene products. But I'm pretty sure the stream of cars zipping by giving us the one finger salute—or hurling a bottle in our direction—had more to do with our hippie hair than the box he was toting.

Under normal circumstances, traveling from Estes to Hays would be about a seven-hour drive, but our trip ended up taking thirty-six hours. You see, when we reached Garden City, Kansas, nobody would pick us up because that's the same general area where the Clutter family was killed in their farm house—the *In Cold Blood* story which had just gripped the nation. Understandably, people were leery of strangers—especially two guys hitchhiking. After a full day of walking, we finally got a ride out of that area and ended up about ten miles from our final destination.

By then, night was fast approaching and we were beyond exhausted. With no jails in sight to enjoy a free bed, we had no choice but to lay down in a ditch by the side of the road for the night. Somehow a young couple driving on the freeway saw us, stopped, and asked if we needed a lift. Luckily, they didn't mind my dog coming along and we arrived home shortly thereafter.

As crazy as our road trip proved to be, in a way it spiked my thirst for adventure and stimulated my openness toward exploring new ideas. Having said that, I'll be the first to admit that not all new ideas are created equal. Need proof? Read on.

BRILLIANT IDEAS THAT HAVE
GONE TO THE DOGS

Believe it or not, there was a time when we manufactured a frame pack for dogs—in three sizes. I assure you we were sober when we thought up that idea. You see, in the early 1970s, backpacking was just starting to become popular across the country. Many of these day-trippers and weekend warriors would take their dogs along with them. We figured if a dog could carry its own food—and maybe a few supplies—a frame pack would be a great idea. And since there appeared to be a need and nobody was filling that need, we decided to make a product that would fill the void. It seemed like a reasonable idea at the time.

As a dog owner myself, I immediately saw the value of a dog frame pack. At that time, I owned an Alaskan malamute by the name of Gombu, named after my friend Nawang Gombu the Sherpa. At two years of age, my dog resembled a small horse, weighing in at a husky 120 pounds. Gombu was strong and loved to pull things, so would hook a ski pole to his collar, and he'd pull me uphill on my cross country skis in the snowy North Cascade mountains.

Gombu also loved to carry things, so we created a pack that fit his back. On one side we

Gombu the dog and Skip.
Photo by Gail Westin.

37

placed a bag with all his dog food. On the other side, we stashed cans of beer. Before long, people brought their dogs to our shop to have them fitted into custom JanSport dog frame packs. Interestingly, some of these customers would come back and say, "Skip, my dog won't go for a walk without his pack!" However, after selling only about a hundred units, we discontinued the dog pack as more important products with a wider appeal surfaced.

The lesson? Not every idea will be a homerun and that's fine. As is often the case, one idea will lead to another, which, in turn, might ultimately produce a really viable concept. By the way, if you can find one of those dog frame packs, they're a real collector's item.

Another idea that appeared great at first but turned out to be unprofitable was the time we opened a JanSport retail store. We started out as a wholesaler—only selling packs to retail outlets and to distributors. My uncle's transmission shop where we were making our frame packs just happened to have a little office up front. When I say little office, this spot was no bigger than maybe a 10' x 12' bedroom. Still, we had this vision of converting it into a hip storefront.

We used old barn wood to cover the walls and thick barn planks to cover the floor. We found a solid pine table that served as our sales counter and nailed a cowbell onto the door to let us know when a customer arrived. We also came across a really cool antique manual brass cash register. We made a JanSport sign, tacked it above the door outside, and were set to go.

Originally, our plan was that nobody would sit in the retail store since we were all so busy in the back hand-making our packs. We figured whoever was free at the time the cowbell rang would go and wait on the customer. In time, we found we would get all of the really hardcore people (as in persnickety) who went first to REI, Eddie Bauer, and the other local specialty places. If they wanted something unique they'd come up to this little new company called JanSport in North Seattle on 175th and Aurora. After a while, we made my sister, Diana, work the store because she could be tough, make the sale, and then get back to work.

One day, we were getting ready to go on a Labor Day weekend trip to the mountains, and our gear was ready to go when a guy came into the store. After spending an hour carefully perusing everything we had, he didn't buy anything. Also, I'm pretty sure he stole my sleeping bag when he left. Frustrated with the retail business, we decided to shut down and spend our time instead on the wholesale side of business. But thankfully, that wasn't the last time we tried a new idea.

39

Skip in the Aurora Avenue retail store.

WHAT'S THE BIG IDEA?

When it comes to brainstorming ways to develop or improve upon a new product, it's been my experience that there are an abundance of *decent* ideas, a number of *good* ideas, and only a few *great* ideas. Perhaps once or twice in a lifetime you'll come face to face with the elusive *breakthrough* idea. The fact that great ideas—and their distant cousin, the breakthrough idea—are rare, should never stop you from testing all ideas. Why? Most of the time, you can't tell when you have a winner until you test it.

Granted, you and your dog might end up stuck in Mexico.

Still, I believe you just have to trust your gut and go for it. You'd think that with the increased waistlines of most Americans, there'd be more gut to trust. Unfortunately, far too many aspiring business leaders have locked their instincts away in a dark broom closet where it won't play with the other kids. That's a mistake. Give yourself permission to chase new ideas—that freedom to explore might just lead you to the next breakthrough product. That's what happened to me in 1972.

As you might remember, school students had no choice but to tote their textbooks and notebooks around campus with their hands. Some tied a belt around them or clutched them to their chest as they walked. Either way, lugging study material was little more than a glorified juggling act—without the pay. There had to be an easier way. But how?

While pondering that conundrum and other mysteries of the universe, I received a phone call from Ed Bergan. Ed was the buyer for the University of Washington campus bookstore. His store carried the usual line of campus-oriented goods, but he also ran a sports shop inside. Ed sold tennis racquets, alpine skis, backpacking gear, and various sports-related items. He also featured our backpacks and daypacks.

That fateful day, Ed said, "Hey Skip, I'm starting to sell your daypacks to our college students who are using them to carry their books. It rains so much here in Seattle, the idea is really catching on. Here's a thought. Why not put something on the bottom of the pack for added support?" Thankfully, I didn't ignore the tug inside of my gut that confirmed Ed might just be onto something. I told him I'd see what we could do.

Meanwhile, Murray and I dug around the shop and stumbled on some extra vinyl. At first, we reinforced the pack bottoms with vinyl. Later we would use leather. We added nylon coil zippers because the metal ones would tend to freeze up. Satisfied with our changes, I called Ed back and told him about our modified design.

Early 1970s daypacks. Photo by Skip Yowell.

He placed an order and then watched in amazement as the packs flew off of his shelves. Wanting to be helpful, Ed called his buddies down in Oregon and Idaho and told them that they should consider selling JanSport packs in their stores because they were a really hot item.

Before long, we started calling on bookstores in the Pacific Northwest. From Ed's initial observation and order, our daypacks started to catch on across the country. Towards the end of the Seventies, many college bookstores were carrying our revised daypacks in stock. By the late Eighties, daypack sales started to catch on at the high school level. Throughout the Nineties, grade school students got in on the action. Today, our daypacks are used worldwide; you can be in the outback of Bhutan, India, or the Himalayas, and you'll find kids going to school carrying a daypack with their books and possessions in it.

Let me leave you with this thought. The words LISTEN and SILENT are both spelled using the same exact six letters. In order to really *listen*, a wise business person remains *silent* while another is speaking. I'm glad I did. After all, the JanSport daypack is *the* product that we are still most known for around the world—with millions of daypacks sold each year. And it's all because of an off-hand idea that didn't fall on deaf ears.

NASTY JACK & KISSING LLAMAS

*H*ere's a pop quiz. What do talking frogs, a drum-playing rabbit, a Spanish-speaking Chihuahua, and a llama that gives kisses have in common? If you guessed that each was the centerpiece of a successful advertising campaign, kindly move to the head of the class. In the event that you're still recovering from the Sixties and, by choice, haven't been paying attention to pop culture, that's cool. I'm referring to the croaking frogs "Bud," "Weis," and "Er," the Energizer bunny, "Gidget," the Taco Bell Chihuahua, and "Cisco," the JanSport llama.

Throughout advertising history, animals have been widely used as company "spokesbeasts" or, in the case of Charlie the Tuna, a "spokesfish." There's something inherently fun about these characters that resonates with consumers. No wonder so many companies spend a king's fortune developing playful ads designed to tap into the inner child in all of us.

When Murray asked me to handle the marketing side of

JanSport back in the early days, we had next to zero dollars for advertising. There wasn't a giant budget for a national ad promotion—with or without cute talking animals. Rather than let that wrinkle trip us up, we did what we always did when confronted by an obstacle: we got creative. Our solution was twofold: *clever catalogs* and *free publicity*.

During the late Sixties and early Seventies, the outdoor industry was in its infancy. Manufacturers and retailers of wilderness gear relied upon catalogs to showcase their wares. Recognizing the value of this must-have tool, our first piece of advertising was the creation of a catalog. But not just any catalog, mind you. Ours had to be different—radically different to attract attention amongst the slick, full color promotional pieces created by the competition. Besides, as I've said previously, if something is worth doing, it's worth having fun with.

Given our connection to the Wild West and the shared rowdy history of our grandfathers, Murray and I decided each catalog would tell a story and it would rely upon a western motif. Those initial catalogs were a real homespun project. Rather than pay professional models to pose with our products, we did the modeling. Murray, Jan, and I would track down the costumes and props, take the pictures, layout the pages, and write the copy.

We worked closely with a local ad agency, Heckler-Bowker, to perfect the process. They also did a couple of things that were instrumental to our growth. Some of the first changes were to merge

Original label and 2nd and 2rd generation of labels.

"Jan Sport" into "JanSport," change the letters to red, and place the name inside of a blue background that resembled a patch. They encouraged us to never change our logo and put it where people could see it. We took their advice seriously and, sure enough, the patch became a very strong trademark for JanSport. Years later, that eye-catching image would become a living billboard on millions and millions of packs. Gotta like that free advertising.

By the way, here's a fun fact from Skip's Almanac—that's my informal collection of random knowledge. In 1971 Heckler-Bowker's co-founder, Gordon Bowker, opened a coffee shop in Seattle with two friends called Starbucks Coffee, Tea, and Spice—better known today as STARBUCKS.

Getting back to our catalogs—long before the advent of computer software programs like Photoshop or Illustrator, we were manipulating photographs by inserting our company logo and ourselves into all sorts of crazy places from yesteryear. You'd find the JanSport trademark on the bow of a boat from the 1890s or on the front of a log cabin hotel in the backwoods of Alaska during the late 1800s. People always got a real chuckle out of those ads because it showed that we, as a company, were having fun even with our advertising.

Like a scene out of the movie *Back to the Future*, it wasn't uncommon for us to land in settings that predated us by a hundred years. From mining camps during the gold rush to old pioneer towns along the Yukon River, you'd see us playing poker, smoking cigars, holstering six-shooters, and making ourselves comfortable by a covered wagon or steam engine train—all with our JanSport packs, tents, luggage, and apparel.

How did we do it? Several steps were involved to doctor the

photographs. First, we identified cool photos from the 1890s in the University of Washington library and secured permission to use them. Then, we'd stage a picture of ourselves dressed up with the appropriate props against a neutral background, also known as a blue wall. Once developed, that image was cut and placed into the original photo and then reshot.

Jan and Skip in an early advertising photo by Marsha Burns.

Sometimes we'd insert just our faces—like in the classic picture of Jan and myself wearing our packs next to several Eskimos as a reindeer munched on a JanSport t-shirt. More often than not, we'd be mingling in a crowd of miners or strolling down the muddy streets amongst the local cattle traders or western roughnecks.

Then again, we sometimes staged the entire western scene rather than insert ourselves into an existing photo. One of my favorites was the "Legend of Nasty Jack." Murray played the part of Nasty Jack while our staff served as the traders. After taking the photo, we grabbed a few beers and went to work on creating a fun storyline to go with it. Here is the folklore we created around Nasty Jack:

After weeks of wandering through miles of virgin wilderness, we finally located Nasty Jack, the legendary trader and fur trapper. Folks is right, he's real nasty. But the sight of all those quality JanSport goods we had for swapping cheered him up right quick. He traded for jackets, packs, and a couple'a tents—he near cleaned us out. Shoot, he was even eyeing my hat! Most likely we'll clear out by tomorrow. Winter sets in mighty quick in these parts and there's a whole bunch'a folks depending on us to outfit 'em before the first snow flies.

47

Nobody could accuse us of failing to have an active imagination! For years, those catalogs were an indispensable part of our marketing. But clever catalogs can only take a company so far. Exposure within the target market-place was the second key to unlocking sales. While we did place a limited number of paid ads during those early years, I worked hard to find as many ways to attract free publicity as possible.

Murray, Phrsumba, and Skip for a "Nasty Jack" photoshoot. Photo by Marsha Burns.

FREE IS GOOD

When it came to free publicity, I managed to get our patented flexible framepack reviewed in several regional publications. But our big break occurred in 1970 with a favorable review in the *Whole Earth Catalog*. Published by Stuart Brand, this behemoth of a catalog was a virtual encyclopedia of recommendations for outdoor gear, back-to-earth products, and environmental issues among other things. Brand and his group of editors searched far and wide to find the best of the best and then highlighted their findings.

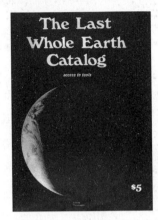

So, it was a really big deal for them to focus their spotlight on us.

We were the first company to create a child-sized framepack. The editors of the *Whole Earth Catalog* thought that was a very cool idea—and said so. Between their positive write-up and the fact that they published our address and phone number, we were slammed with interest. Cards and letters poured in from around the country. Some were from consumers and some were from proprietors of outdoor equipment shops interested in carrying our Mini framepack. You can't easily buy that kind of exposure.

Several years later, in 1973, we invited Steve Netherby, a writer for *Field & Stream*, to join us on a hike in the North Cascades. He agreed and participated in what was admittedly a strenuous hike. Murray and I provided dome tents and our innovative JanSport framepacks, which were different than anything Steve had seen or used. Duly impressed, Steve returned to his office and wrote a fantastic article entitled, "Who is JanSport?"

Once again, we enjoyed a fresh wave of exposure at a time when we didn't have an advertising budget to support a national campaign. Free plugs such as these from industry trade magazines definitely made a difference in our bottom line. In my view, anytime you can get people reading or talking about your product, you've created promotional value—which, for a hungry hippie, is cheap advertising.

TANGLED UP IN TANG

In keeping with the pursuit of free publicity, I was constantly on the lookout for ways to enhance the word-of-mouth awareness of JanSport products. It occurred to me that the quickest way to ramp up the peer-to-peer promotion of our goods was to make the best product money can buy and then surpass the customer's expectation with a surprise, add-on feature, like hiding a tote bag inside a piece of a JanSport luggage. Customers who buy the suitcase only later learn—perhaps packing for a trip—that there's a neat tote bag folded into a secret compartment to use for the return trip if needed. People love to be surprised like that and frequently tell a friend about their cool experience with a JanSport product.

Here's another example of adding value—one that nearly backfired on us. I was meeting with a contact at *Backpacker* magazine who, I learned, was engaged in talks with the manufacturer of Tang—the orange powder drink mix. Tang had been used by the astronauts on the moon, but was having some difficulty entering the orbit of the outdoor community. My friend at *Backpacker* was pitching their magazine as a great way for Tang to be introduced to the outdoor market.

That's when I had a vision. What if we put a package of Tang into each backpack? Tang would get great exposure directly with hikers, trekkers, and climbers. JanSport would get to provide an added little surprise in every product sold—at no cost to us. It appeared to be a great idea, and evidently, the folks at Tang concurred. Several months later, I was on the road meeting with some of our dealers when I received a panicked phone call from the manager of our warehouse in Paine Field, Washington.

Evidently, a huge eighteen-wheeler pulled up to the loading dock stuffed to the ceiling with Tang. I knew space in our warehouse was tight at best, but now we were awash in cases of Tang . . . literally *thousands* of cases of Tang. In my defense, I had no earthly idea that we'd be receiving so many free samples to distribute—but it was absolutely no consolation to the good folks working in the warehouse. What's worse is the fact that there was no way we could use all of it before the expiration date on the individual foil packets.

I ended up giving Lou Whittaker of Rainier Mountaineering, Inc. hundreds of boxes of Tang to use during his guided climbs of Mt. Rainier. Tang got their exposure to outdoor-types, while Lou, his RMI guides, and guests, drank Tang for several years at Camp Muir. Maybe that's why Lou's complexion looked a little orange the last time I saw him.

KISSING LLAMAS FOR FUN AND PROFITS

The year was 1982. I was poolside working on a serious Coppertone tan and nursing a margarita when a woman unknown to me approached. I shielded the sun from my face and, with a squint, noticed a man standing in her shadow. The place was a hotel somewhere in Southern California where I was attending a dealer rep event. The woman must have noticed the look of bewilderment on my face because she promptly extended her hand and hastily introduced herself as Andrea Gabbard.

Andrea was a writer for *Outdoor Retailer* magazine. Her colleague sold ads for the publication, although Andrea appeared to take the lead in making their pitch. While I don't recall whether or not I bought an ad at that time, our paths would cross again in 1986. A mutual friend and accomplished photographer, Keith Gunnar, his wife Antje, Andrea Gabbard, and I decided to plan a trip to hell. Hells Canyon National Recreation Area, that is.

Hugging the Snake River between Oregon and Idaho, Hells Canyon is the deepest river gorge in North America—deeper than the Grand Canyon by 2,000 feet. This sensational wilderness encompasses 652,488 acres of indescribable beauty while plunging more than 8,000 feet below the He Devil Peak of Idaho's Seven Devils Mountains. While no cars are allowed, there's plenty of hiking, horseback riding, and world-class white water rafting to satisfy the restless soul.

We were part of the first commercial llama-packing excursion into the canyon—sort of a test drive, prototype trip authorized by the park. It was believed that llamas were more environmentally friendly and would do less damage to the trails. Aside from measuring the ecological impact of the llamas, Keith and I would be shooting photos of JanSport gear for an upcoming advertising spread, while Andrea would be penning an article for *Outdoor Retailer*.

With bags packed and cameras in tow, we embarked on a

51

seven day trip—the four of us, two llama packers, and six llamas. Interestingly, the first leg of our voyage was on a jet boat since there are no bridges or roads across the ten mile wide expanse of the canyon. Much to my amazement, the guides had no difficulty leading the llamas across the gangplank and onto the stern. Without hesitation, each llama tucked its legs under its body and sat down on the deck as if they had just strolled onto Noah's Ark.

Much could be said about spending a week in Hells Canyon, including the time we found ourselves navigating a one-foot wide trail that arched about 500 feet above the river bed before descending to our camp. Loose rock covered the dirt trail making passage as hard as, well, hell. Each of us clutched a llama's lead rope. Sure-footed and endlessly patient with their human travelers, the llamas would slow to a snail's pace to allow us to pick our way. The lead llama stopped several times and craned his neck back to look at his charges. Satisfied with our progress, he'd snort, then turn and continue on his way.

Perhaps the most memorable discovery of the week was learning that one llama in particular named Cisco was exceptionally frisky. Always quick with a kiss, Cisco's lip smacking personality gave me another vision: *What if Keith could capture a photo of Cisco and me puckering up?* That

Cisco the llama and Skip in Hells Canyon, Idaho. Photo by Keith Gunnar.

could be used in a cool print ad. I shared the idea with Keith who agreed it was worth a shot.

We needed to rehearse the photograph several times. For their part, Andrea and Antje were hooting and hollering so much that they kept breaking Cisco's concentration. After all, I'm sure I had to be the first hippie to steal a smooch, and I think Cisco was still getting comfortable with the whole idea.

In the end, we managed to capture a wonderfully playful photograph that became the basis for a full-page JanSport ad. Granted, Cisco's notability never rose to the level of, say, Tony the Tiger hawking Kellogg's Frosted Flakes. And, unlike the meteoric launch of Budweiser's Spuds McKenzie as a pop culture icon, Cisco never got to bask in the glow of a Super Bowl ad campaign. Still, we got a ton of mileage out of that quirky promotion.

53

BUTTON PUSHER: THE FOUR GREAT DIRECTIONS

The majority of the free advertising and promotions we pursued were designed to reach a broad market. There was, however, an idea I had which translated into a cool "inner circle" incentive for our dealers and employees. I had been reading a book called *Seven Arrows* which explored the philosophy of the Plains Indian tribes. Their beliefs seemed consistent with the harmony of spirit that we hippies were seeking, which is why it struck a chord with me.

Halfway through the book, I had a vision. I immediately called Dan and Jill Anderson who specialized in handmade jewelry and told them about my concept. I wanted them to make a pin based upon the idea of the Indian heritage I had been reading about. Together we designed a logo called the "Four Great Directions" which they, in turn, fashioned into a distinctive pin. This colorful keepsake symbolized the strength of character and the adventurous spirit consistent with our Indian forerunners.

Over the years, I awarded a handful of the pins to JanSport dealers who had really gotten behind the product or to employees who had gone above and beyond the call of duty. I'd present these awards at different key moments, mostly at sales meetings or trade shows. Within the brotherhood of the outdoor industry, that pin became a Hallmark of achievement and is worn with pride to this day by the thirty or forty people I've felt were totally committed enough to earn it. The "Four Great Directions" pin is a great example of how a simple idea can yield great results.

54

I can honestly say that when it comes to advertising, money can sometimes be a crutch. Furthermore, too much money can actually stifle your creativity. How? When you're flush with cash, you're not always hungry enough to push the boundaries and find a creative solution. I'm not opposed to having lots of cash for advertising, mind you. But without the luxury of a fat bank account back then, Murray, Jan, and I were pushed to find another way.

We knew we had the best darn pack money could buy, but

"Four Great Directions" logo design by Dan and Jill Anderson and Skip Yowell.

going door-to-door seemed both unhippieish and a slow way to get the word out about our packs. Without significant marketing dollars to work with, we were backed into a corner. The best way out was to put our creative juices on maximum spin. Truthfully, if we had it to do all over, I don't think I would have changed a thing.

Okay, maybe one thing . . . I would love to have seen Cisco the Llama go head-to-head with Joe Camel in a spitting contest. That event would have made for some great pictures.

55

MAGIC MOUNTAIN

*I*f I were to pinpoint a watershed moment in the history of JanSport, I'd point to February of 1971. At the time, we were selling backpacks to a sports shop in Tacoma, Washington called Whittaker's Chalet. I had met the proprietor, Lou Whittaker, several years prior and found him to be instantly likeable, even though he was a tough mountaineer. When I say Lou was tough, he was the kind of breed that's part mountain man and part cowboy. Tall, lanky, and tougher than beef jerky, Lou was a spirited horse that refused to be tamed.

Lou launched his guide service Rainier Mountaineering, Inc. in 1968, having obtained the official guide concession from the Park Service. During the summer, Whittaker's Chalet sold mountaineering and backpacking gear. In the winter, Lou ran a ski school along with RMI's guide service up 14,410 feet to Mt. Rainier's peak. Clearly, his boundless energy and passion for mountain climbing runs in the family. His twin brother Jim Whittaker was the first American to summit Mt. Everest.

That January, I called Lou and arranged to conduct a JanSport in-store clinic for his employees. After our presentation, Lou, Murray, and I hung out and talked shop. Whenever I met with customers, I tried to learn as much as I could about their operation so that I could do a better job of servicing their specific needs. The more we spoke, the more I admired Lou's love of adventure and his unmatched entrepreneurial spirit.

At one point in the conversation, Lou described his plans for the first RMI winter climbing seminar on Mt. Rainier. That got our attention and Murray and I signed up on the spot. The thought of scaling the second highest and most heavily glaciated mountain in the continental U.S. with Lou seemed like such a cool idea. Plus, it would be a great excuse to test our gear under some intense conditions. Neither of us knew that what we were about to experience would change the course of history for JanSport.

OVER THE TOP

I'm a competitive person by nature. Once I made the commitment to join Lou Whittaker's winter seminar, I knew I had to be able to go the distance. To turn back once I started the climb was not in my makeup. Murray felt the same way. We decided to train hard for the trip and be 100% physically in shape. We also needed to scrap together the necessary gear and supplies, including a set of snow shoes which we didn't own. That's when an interesting thing happened.

As we trained and talked with others who had climbed Rainier,

*Murray Pletz and the blue van on
Mt. Rainier. Photo by Skip Yowell.*

we found ourselves immediately
brainstorming new designs and
new items that could be used
on the trip, *before* the trip even
happened—ones that might be a
little better than what was
available on the market. As I've
seen time and again, whenever
we took such calculated risks
instead of remaining within the
safe zone with our experiences,
new concepts emerged that benefited our business.

59

When the time for the trip finally came, we stuffed our gear
into the blue Dodge van and headed to Seattle. With Dylan
belting out songs on the 8-track, my mind drifted back to the
first time I stood at the foot of Mt. Rainier. I was in junior high
at the time and was spending the summer with Murray. I mar-
veled at how Rainier could stand so tall with virtually nothing
around it. This member of the Cascade Range, I had learned,
sported twenty-seven massive glaciers and was named after Rear
Admiral Peter Rainier by Captain George Vancouver in 1792.

As a teenager, I can't say I ever dreamed of standing on
Rainier's breathtaking summit. That idea was just too far out to
imagine. It was simply the most impressive mountain I had ever
seen. Even as Murray and I drove that afternoon, I found myself
wondering whether or not I'd keep pace with the rest of the
climbers. The mountain was unbelievably massive. My plan was

to stay right on the heels of Lou because there was no way that I wanted to get lost, and I was determined to make the summit no matter what.

Murray and I parked our van at the park ranger's station in Paradise, Washington. We unloaded our framepacks and snow-shoes then caught up with the others. Lou began by teaching us the basics of snow travel, belays, self-arrest, and how to make igloos and shelters out of blocks of ice into an A-frame if we needed to get out of the elements. His confidence and knowledge was reassuring. We were in good hands. Even so, nothing we had heard could prepare us for the Wrath of Rainier.

You've probably heard the adage, "Anything that can possi-bly go wrong, will go wrong." That sums up our first big moun-tain climb. Though things started out just fine, the expedition rapidly became a real disaster. Why? The winds rapidly shifted from a gentle breeze to that of an icy cold blast. And, as it turned out, our trip just happened to be conducted the same year that Mt. Rainier set the world's record for snowfall—a full 1,122 inches of snow. For those who prefer their misery measured in feet, that's 93 feet of new snow. I learned about that bit of trivia the hard way.

We spent nine grueling hours snowshoeing our way up 10,000 feet to Camp Muir, which was little more than a rugged staging area for summit climbers, the centerpiece being a wooden hut with bunk beds and an ice covered floor. It didn't matter though. We were beat from lugging our heavy packs and rest was the first order of business.

Just as we were getting the camp settled, something really provoked the winds. The gusts were unbelievable; they whipped

60

around with more fury than a Jimi Hendrix guitar solo. We were broadsided by a white-out so severe, I could barely see my hand in front of my face.

On a practical level, Lou instructed us to tie a rope between the hut and the outhouse, a rickety structure some fifty paces away. That's how bad it was. We literally had to hold on to the rope to get over to the outhouse to take care of business. If going to the bathroom was *that* difficult, I thought there was no way we could reach the summit. The larger issue that crossed my mind was whether or not we'd make it out alive.

Nevertheless, and at Lou's suggestion, we lingered at Camp Muir for several days hoping for a break in the weather. We waited and waited. When the blizzard refused to relent, Lou had to bring us down on altimeter and compass-bearings alone, some-thing that only a seasoned guide could do. As Lou always says, "The climb is only half over. You've got to get down safely for it to count." Speaking of which, one of my borrowed snowshoes broke during our return. That served as a valuable lesson: dependable gear is not a luxury—it might just save your life.

After several hours of fighting the high winds and a violent snowstorm, we managed to descend to the Paradise Ranger Station (elevation 5,400 feet) where we had parked our cars several days earlier. All Murray and I could think of was jumping in, firing up the heater, and thawing out our toes. But the cars were gone. I blinked to make sure my mind wasn't playing tricks on me. Sure enough, there were no cars in sight.

That's when Murray spied the roof of our blue van peeking out from under a massive blanket of snow. Upon further inspection, we found all of our vehicles buried under at least six feet of the

61

fresh white stuff. Our situation went from bad to worse. Sizing up our options, Lou explained that the only way off of the mountain would be to get a snow plow from Longmire (2,761 feet) to clear the road and to dig out our cars. We went to the ranger station but found nobody there.

The unflappable Lou who spent years on numerous search and rescue missions, used the radio to call down to the rangers at Longmire who, thankfully, sent the help we needed. Several hours later, we began to drive from our frozen Paradise to Longmire.

About halfway down the mountain, the pale sun traded places with a frosty moon. Darkness settled on the mountain like a thick, black cloak. It was at that precise time and place where the van's battery died. Checking a map, Murray and I figured we were a good ten miles from Longmire. With the winds still more cantankerous than a junkyard dog, we knew there was no way we were going to get out and start walking.

Exhausted, cold, and famished as hell, we took inventory of our situation. We determined that we had a few sunflower seeds and that was all. We longed for a shower since we absolutely stunk after sleeping and trekking in the same socks and clothes for an entire week. But the worst part was the realization that without a working battery, we couldn't listen to the radio in the van. Thankfully, we didn't have to become a couple of freeze-dried stiffs before help arrived. When the rest of the team realized our van hadn't come down, they sent up the Snowcat—a specialized snow tractor with caterpillar-type tracks for wheels—to rescue us. We reached Longmire at about 1 A.M.

I'd like to say that was the end of the nightmare. But it wasn't.

Murray and I didn't have any money on us so we couldn't check into the lodge with the others. Desperate for a warm spot to catch some rest, we noticed that the lodge had an outdoor bathroom which was a separate cinder block building parked next to the lodge. While sleeping in a bathroom might sound gross, at least it was out of the elements and it was warm—make that *reasonably* warm, certainly not toasty warm. We pulled our sleeping bags from the van and called it a night.

Just as I was about to fall asleep, I heard a voice. An employee came into the bathroom at about 1:30 A.M. and stumbled upon us. When he asked what we were doing, I gave him the *Reader's Digest* version of what we had just been through and said that we couldn't check into the lodge because we didn't have any money. He said, "Well, it's not normal, but you can come up and stay in my room. It's awful cold in here." Thankful for at least one break, we took our sleeping bags up to his room.

Turning out the lights, he said, "Look, guys, I'll probably get in trouble if they see you coming down in the morning. It's probably better if they didn't know you stayed up here. If you could, take the outside steps down when you leave." We assured him that was the least we could do, and we did as promised.

However, the next day as we were about halfway down the second flight of stairs, we hit a snag. The staircase came into the direct view of a huge picture window adjacent to the fireplace and the fireplace was busy warming a room full of people who suddenly watched two sleeping-bag-toting hippies slink down the stairs. So much for our secret escape.

63

A MOUNTAIN OF POSSIBILITIES

You might be wondering whether the trip was worth the risks and hassles. Without hesitation, I'd say yes. Murray and I came away from that winter climb changed in several ways. We were made stronger through the adversity of this experience because we were stretched beyond our comfort zones. But aside from those more obvious truths, we found out we had more resourcefulness, perseverance, and courage than we ever imagined. Incidentally, all three are needed to successfully climb the corporate ladder . . . or any other personal challenge you may face.

Additionally, we became more dedicated to crafting the best possible outdoor gear with our fledging company and knew that we had what it took to overcome any boundary. Against this back-drop, the watershed idea emerged. We wondered, *What if Lou would agree to lead a JanSport climb up Mt. Rainier for our dealers? What if they, too, might benefit from such an adrenaline-*

JanSport dealer climb on Mt. Rainier. Photo by Keith Gunnar.

pumping adventure? Nobody had ever done it. Nobody was doing it. So why not us?

Although we were selling our gear to outdoor stores throughout the Pacific Northwest, many of their sales people had never experienced mountain climbing. We figured if our dealers climbed with us, they'd see our product in action, they'd experience what their customers experience, and they would have an opportunity to communicate with each other and trade ideas. We pitched our brainstorm to Lou. Not only did he agree to lead the JanSport climb, he offered to use his guide service team to support the effort.

As we'd soon discover, the JanSport-sponsored dealer climb emerged as a key component in our marketing effort. With Lou's help, this annual event became a unique opportunity that JanSport offered unlike any other company in our field. From our point of view, the dealers would go back to their stores knowing much more about the gear they were selling, and, at the very least, have a phenomenal experience.

Back at the office, Murray and I got busy. We started by planning a program for the week-long event. On Sunday, participants would get a tour of the JanSport factory to see our operation. For dinner, dining aboard a boat on the Puget Sound sounded like a great way for thirty or so people to break the ice. Monday morning we'd get everyone fitted with their gear at the Paradise Guide House before heading up Mt. Rainier to acclimatize at Camp Muir. Tuesday and Wednesday we'd teach a variety of skills—crevasse rescue, ice climbing, cave building, rope management—the works. Of course, we'd build in extra time for general fun.

Thursday was the big day when we planned to go, weather

65

permitting, to the summit. According to Lou, we needed to get up at four o'clock in the morning because the snow would become slushy as the day went on and climbers are prone to slipping and sliding under those conditions. In the early hours, the snow is firm and allows for better traction. Under normal conditions, we could make the five hour final climb and be back at Camp Muir just after lunch. Finally, after teaching a few additional skills on Friday, the team would descend.

To cap things off, we decided to schedule a big dinner dance party where we could eat, drink, and hand out awards. At that point, we were ready to go. We felt sure we had designed the most perfectly challenging, exhilarating, frustrating, maddening, and meaningful week our dealers would ever experience. Satisfied with the plan, we mailed the flyers and, to our delight, dealer interest surpassed our expectations.

To make a long story short, we had a fabulous debut climb. Future dealer seminars sold out quickly. We even went through a period of time where we had to have two climbs because we were turning away so many people.

As of 2006, we've hosted the JanSport Mt. Rainier dealer seminar for thirty-four years in a row. Looking back, we've probably escorted close to a thousand people up that magical mountain.

TAKING IT TO THE EXTREME

There are serious risks associated with climbing. I fully recognize that a lot of companies would shy away because of the inherent dangers. Fearful of a potential lawsuit, they'd opt for something less risky. However, I've always felt that it's just as dangerous climbing behind the wheel of a car as it can be on a mountain.

Let me ask you a question. Are you a person who takes risks, or do you play it safe?

By risks, I'm not talking about recklessly throwing caution to the wind or needlessly endangering life and limb. But let's face the facts. The default position of most people, including many in business, is to play it safe when confronted by a new opportunity, idea, dream, or direction. They'll hit the brakes, they hedge the bet, or they consult with a "risk manager" to minimize their exposure if the gamble goes sour. In the end, far too many people are paralyzed by fear, whether it be the fear of the unknown, fear of failure, fear of being misunderstood, fear of injury or loss, or the fear of fear itself.

Rather than reap the rich rewards that are a byproduct of taking a calculated risk, we're tempted to take the safe, predictable route. We prefer the darkness inside of the cocoon rather than the

joy of flight that only comes to those who break out and test their wings. I'm grateful that in 1971 Lou invited me to take a risk and skate outside of the lines. What's keeping you from doing the same?

1971: Lou Whittaker at Camp Muir at 10,000 feet.

67

TAKING CARE
OF BUSINESS

A byproduct of being in business for forty years is that I've worked with a diverse range of businesses. I've come to learn, sometimes the hard way, that each corporate culture is exactly that—a *culture*. To survive, the earnest employee does his or her best to understand both the written and unwritten rules that make their corporate environment unique.

At JanSport, we've always been about incorporating fun in everything we do. Life is such a grand adventure. Why waste it doing something you dislike, right? If we had wanted a regular job with all of the usual corporate trappings, Murray, Jan, and I could have applied at any number of big employers in Seattle. But making all of the money in the world without enjoying yourself in the process just wasn't appealing to us. We wanted work to be both creative and *fun*. Making money was a plus.

For example, in the early days if we invented a new backpack, we'd close the office and go hiking and climbing to test the pack in the wilderness. Probably half of the stuff we dreamed up was products designed for us to have a better experience in the great outdoors. Since we were having such a good time perfecting our products, those who bought them would, in turn, have more fun. We became known as the hippies who added fun to the function.

That carefree attitude was evident in the shop, too. We'd dress casually—as in bell bottoms, cut-off shorts, and fringe jackets. It didn't have to be a Friday for my brother, Randy, and Murray to play guitars during a break or at the end of the day. And we'd play loud music after work. Not only was our work culture a fun, playful environment, we enjoyed each other.

Many evenings after work, we'd wander across the street to Parker's Ballroom. We knew the bouncer would let us in for free (since we didn't have any money), and we'd dance and listen to the likes of Paul Revere and the Raiders. And, candidly, there were times when we'd drink the beers other people left on the table when they'd get up to dance.

Naturally, when you had as much fun as we did, it was difficult to get too disheartened over the petty stuff that far too many corporate cultures seem to obsess over. I believe this is also known as corporate politics. Personally, I never could understand the mind games, the kissing-up and schmoozing, and the being in the loop—or out of the loop as needed—that is frequently part of the office scene. In my view, I should treat each person I meet with genuine respect, a receptive ear, and kindness, which is why one of our corporate mottos for the last four decades has been: *Take your business seriously, not yourself.*

That being said, I'll never forget an occasion when we lost sight of this principle.

GETTING THE BOOT IN SAN FRANCISCO

We got a call from Gorin Brothers, a distributor in San Francisco, who was interested in carrying our packs. This would have been in 1970 and JanSport was still a relatively small outfit. While excited about the prospect of expanding the distribution of our packs, we couldn't afford the air fare from Seattle to San Francisco. However, when we learned that Janis Joplin and Big Brother & the Holding Company were scheduled to appear in the bay area, we knew we just *had* to find a way there.

I know it sounds crazy to be more motivated by a cool concert than a business prospect, but somehow enjoying life and having fun always managed to be a priority. We decided to drive the sixteen hours for the concert—and meet with the distributor while in town.

After we confirmed with Gorin Brothers that we'd be coming, Murray and I looked at each other as the realization hit us: this would be our first official business road trip and we didn't own suits. Our wardrobes were primarily an assortment of cut-off shorts, t-shirts, and hiking boots. Of course, we could have just gone dressed as the flower power hippies we were. But we didn't. Call it a momentary lapse of judgment or maybe a brief dose of bad karma.

Whatever the reason, we became a little self-conscious about having the right business look. We decided to hunt down dress clothes for the trip. I got a hold of a double-breasted, blue suit with gray pinstripes from Nordstrom, complete with the extra wide lapel that could double as a set of tent flaps. The blue shirt and tie were borderline claustrophobic, but at least I looked like a quasi-businessman. For Murray's part, he managed to find a brown suede blazer and matching brown vest, gray pinstriped pants, a light green shirt and a black string bowtie. So rare was this occasion, Jan even took a photo to document the moment. Decked out in our new threads, we hit the road.

After we arrived in San Francisco, we made our first presentation at the Gorin Brothers' office. Liking what they saw—with our product line, not necessarily our suits—they placed an order. As we left, thought struck us that we might as well call on a few other shops before the concert. We dropped in on a North Face store in San Francisco that also decided to carry our pack line.

Encouraged by these sales, we stopped by Sierra Designs in Berkeley, another outdoor retailer, who didn't place an order. But still, selling product to two out of three new accounts wasn't a bad day's work. After checking our watches, we figured we could squeeze in one more cold call. If we hustled, there'd still be time to change out of our suits and into our real clothes in the back of our blue van before the concert.

When we stopped by the Ski Hut, an interesting thing happened. We showed up in our business attire and walked confidently to the register. After asking to speak with the owner, we were directed to the back of the storefront to see Peter Noone. As we moved through the store, the employees started giving us

these shocked looks as if we belonged in the freak show at the circus. I overheard one person say, "What, *those* are the JanSport guys?"

Murray and Skip on their first business trip to San Francisco.

Maybe they were stunned by our Elvis-sized sideburns, shoulder-length hair, or Murray's goatee. I do know that they thought our product with its flexible frame design was too radical. You know, too far out on the edge at a time when all other packs on the market used ridged frames. In the end, they just couldn't get past the fact that we were hippies trying to enter the business world. They literally threw us out of their store!

Frankly, we weren't too bummed out. As Janis Joplin would sing later that night, "Freedom is just another word for nothing left to lose." In other words, in our hearts we knew we were all about freedom—freedom to express ourselves, to be ourselves, and to pursue things like adventure, discovery and fun. That's who we were *inside* regardless of what clothes we wore on the outside.

Looking back I realized that, for a brief moment, we attempted to become people we were not in order to appeal to what we *thought* was the corporate culture of those whom we would contact. Sure, we had the suits, but we were not businessmen in the traditional sense. To pretend otherwise was to be unfaithful to who we really were—slightly irreverent hippies on a mission to make the best packs in the world. That was one of the last times we wore those monkey suits, although it wasn't the last time I got in trouble with the fashion police.

DRESSED FOR SUCCESS

In 1972, Cummins, Inc. of Columbus, Indiana, the parent company of K2, acquired JanSport. During the acquisitions process, I met and came to work closely with Dan McConnell, who served as an assistant to the vice chairman of the board. One of Dan's assignments was to take ten percent of Cummins profits to identify and purchase companies who were not into heavy manufacturing like Cummins.

Ideally, Dan would find emerging companies who were ranked second, third, or fourth in their class but that demonstrated strong potential to move up. Obviously, Cummins was banking on the prospect that these newly acquired companies would rocket into first place—if given a little extra cash and perhaps some fresh management direction.

The first company they bought was K2 Skis. At the time of purchase, K2 was eighth in their field and specialized in a new fiberglass ski design. The industry leader was HEAD who made metal skis in those days. Within three years, K2 became the number one company and was worth much more than Cummins had paid for it. What Cummins realized after owning K2 for about a year was that K2 sold skis a season ahead of time. In other words, they made skis in the summer and delivered them in the fall. But during the winter there was no real action with the company.

Chuck Ferris at K2 knew about the JanSport company, which led to acquisition talks spearheaded by Dan McConnell. You see,

JanSport fit perfectly into the K2 business-cycle hole. We sold our products in the winter for people to use in the summer. By putting the two companies together, Dan knew K2-Cummins would have a strong revenue stream flowing all year long. Dan hopped on a plane and

Skip during a Mt. Rainier seminar.
Photo by Keith Gunnar.

flew to Seattle to check out our operation. He was in for the shock of his life.

For starters, the Cummins corporation had *serious* dress code issues. Dan, as well as all male employees, were required to wear white shirts, preferably starched, and a tie all of the time—they even had a rule that you couldn't wear a blue shirt. No exceptions! Regarding hair, men had two choices: it had to be cropped close or buzzed off. Period. To say that the Cummins' culture was ultra-conservative would be an understatement.

As the corporate guy assigned to be the liaison between our companies, Dan immediately saw that there was a huge gap—better make that a gap on par with the Grand Canyon—between JanSport and his corporate world, even aside from the matter of a dress code. For instance, the Cummins headquarters was a specially designed office utilizing cubicles, a relatively newfangled idea at the time. Each employee was situated in their "creative work space"—which was nothing more than a ten-by-ten foot slice of a cookie cutter maze of tan and gray partitions. Indeed, Cummins was a highly regulated work environment; anything you tacked onto the bulletin board had to be approved by the Committee. It was just that kind of uptight place.

When Dan came to see us, we had about forty employees all working in casual clothing. There wasn't a suit or tie to be found—except for what he was wearing. Nor was there a committee to approve postings on the bulletin board. In spite of these radical differences, Cummins purchased JanSport, after which Dan encouraged me to travel to Columbus to meet some of the folks back at headquarters. He figured it would be a good idea to put a name and a face together now that we were going to be

75

joined at the hip. Besides, Cummins needed to know more about JanSport and I was just the guy to tell the JanSport story. Several weeks later, at the request of Phil Clement, the President of Cummins, I flew to Indiana.

Dan was waiting in his creative work space for me to show up. As it got later and later in the morning, I'm sure he had to wonder whether or not I'd make it. I did, and this time I left the suit at home. As I worked my way through the jungle of partitions, I heard people exhaling, as if winded from a five-mile run. Just over the tops of the flimsy walls, I could see Dan's head pop up in the distance. From his perspective, about all he would have seen is my shoulder length blonde hair, a pretty serious tan, and a big Foo Manchu mustache—from the neck up, I'm sure I looked like a California surfer. Talk about a real scandal!

As I wandered to the far corner of the floor, people were standing up and looking at me with a mixture of fascination and deep concern. I'm sure they were worried that I hadn't received the memo about not wearing jeans—JEANS, of all things—Cummins would never, ever permit an employee to wear jeans to work. My really nice pair of cowboy boots and a white, fringed leather jacket were likewise forbidden. At least I was wearing a white shirt, albeit opened and unbuttoned half way down my chest.

To top it off, I wore a huge, squash blossom necklace picked up from Arizona or some such outpost of humanity. Yes, my attire literally took their breath away. As Dan would tell me later, they were all trying to figure out three things: Who was I? Where was I, this freak of nature going? And what did I want at Cummins?

I finally made it to Dan's desk, sat down, and started to talk about business. While we were visiting, I couldn't help but notice how everybody suddenly had to go to the copier which just happened to be located a few steps beyond Dan's cubical. Evidently, my presence became the talk of the town. Did I know that I was out of synch with those around me? Sure. But after the San Francisco trip, I learned it was always better to be who I was by expressing myself rather than attempting to be someone or *something* I wasn't—and let the chips fall as they may. Remember, take your business seriously, not yourself. It's freeing—albeit controversial at times.

Case in point. After a long day at Cummins, Dan, his wife, another associate from Cummins, and I went out to eat. Since we left directly from work, Dan and his buddy were wearing their standard starched white shirts, ties, and suits. We went to a place called The Brown County Inn. This was a local eatery that has served their famous hot biscuits, apple butter and other Midwestern traditional offerings for decades, and one of those spots where the waitresses stay forever. Our waitress had worked there for twenty-five years.

While I don't recall her name, I'll never forget the exchange. After she announced the specials, she asked us for our drink order—starting with the nicely-dressed folks from Cummins. The others ordered a beer or a glass of wine after which the waitress turned to me. I offered a smile. She peered at me over the top edge of her glasses like a miffed librarian because my book was overdue. She said, "So, what are you having?"

I said, "I'd like a red beer, please."

The waitress folded her arms and shot me a wary glance. Unsure if she heard me, I repeated the request. She said, "Sir, we have Miller, we have Bud, and we have Miller Lite, but we don't serve no Commie beer here."

Commie beer? Puzzled, I said, "I'm not talking about Commie beer, ma'am. I asked for a *red* beer."

She said, "I'm telling you, we don't have it."

Trying to be helpful, I said, "It's just beer and tomato juice. All you do is put a little tomato juice in the bottom of the glass and fill it the rest of the way with beer. Maybe a dash of Tabasco sauce and a pinch of salt if you have them."

She winced and puckered her face as if she'd been sprayed by a skunk. "I won't make that. I'm not doing that. It's very *odd*. I'm not gonna serve you that. Like I said, we don't serve no Commie beer here."

Not wanting to make any more of a scene, I finally said, "Okay, then I'll just have a Bud." So much for pleasing the customer! For the rest of the meal, the waitress made it clear she was miffed at my request.

In some ways, this dear soul was no different than the folks at Cummins. Both had difficulty overcoming the fact I was so different, so out of the norm. And yet, as the folks at Cummins would discover in time, I was actually an okay guy—long hair and all.

In the end, the combination of K2-Cummins and JanSport proved to be a very successful partnership that would last for about five years. After that period of time, their corporate strategy changed and Cummins decided to divest themselves of all the properties they had acquired. As for JanSport, I knew our winning strategy was a relaxed corporate culture, and we'd always be successful as long as we were a team that took our business seriously, not ourselves.

Now, if you'll excuse me, I think I'll find some place where I can order a red beer.

8

ALMOST DEAD AND THE ORIGINAL DOME TENT

*B*e glad when things don't work out as planned. You might just discover the next great invention. I should know. It happened to us on more than one occasion. In this case, what started out as a simple cross-country ski trip with a photographer from the *Seattle Times*, turned out to be a journey that would revolutionize the way tents are made around the world. Of course, at the time, we didn't see things that way. We were just concerned that our attempt to impress the press almost got us killed.

Here's what happened. Back in 1971, we were still a small, home-grown company. We were also exploring the development of our own A-frame tent. Unfortunately, we didn't have a marketing department—nor could we afford a fancy advertising campaign—to introduce our version of the traditional tent. We figured the best way to get exposure for our packs and new prototype JanSport tent was to have a professional news photographer catching us and our equipment in action. Nothing like getting some free press, right? At least that was our big idea.

Murray, Jan, and I scheduled a three-day, 21-mile cross-country ski trip from Mission Ridge in Wenatchee to Liberty, a cool little ghost town near Blewett Pass in Washington's Cascade Mountains. Ski guide Chuck Cross agreed to lead the way. Joining us were several business associates from REI, Gary Rose and Dave Chantler, as well as Ira Spring, the photographer, who was working on a pictorial feature for the *Seattle Times*. Privately, we thought this might just lead to our big break. You know, a well-placed story with a few awesome photos in the mountains could put the JanSport tent and packs on the map. Everything was going as planned, except for the one thing that nobody had control over: the weather.

After a vigorous first day on the trail, we stopped to set up camp for the night. It was the dead of winter and, as is often the case in the Cascade Mountains, the mercury dropped like a rock. The temperature hit a bone-chilling minus five degrees. In fact, it was so cold that Ira managed to take just one picture before the shutter on his camera froze. With the winds developing a nasty attitude and the sun in a hurry to set, we raced to assemble our prototype A-frame tent.

Making matters worse, it started to snow. This was not a gentle, "It's beginning to look a lot like Christmas" snow, one that would make us look like hardy outdoorsmen for Ira's photo spread. No. I'm talking about a raging, mad-as-hell, "Get off my mountain" blizzard that gusted and pelted us from all sides. Our mustaches and hair were quickly covered in ice. As it turned out, the only picture Ira snapped on that trip was of our frosted mustaches and hair. All we could do was take cover—and *fast*.

Ira and the REI team took to their tents while the three of us squeezed into our tent. Once safely inside, Murray fired up the portable stove to make coffee to thaw us out while making a much needed dinner for nourishment. But the wind seemed to have an agenda of its own; the relentless, uninvited gusts of frozen air forced its way through the walls of our tent seeking to snuff out the flame of our stove. We struggled to protect the flame in those cramped quarters, but in spite of our efforts, the stove was extinguished. Our hot meal was put on ice.

Without a source of heat, we huddled together doing our best to stay warm. About three o'clock in the morning the zipper on the tent door broke, launching the door flap into an immediate and rapid spasm. The wind-whipped snow gladly swirled inside the new opening. Then, the tent pole which had secured the door was yanked from its moorings and began to spin around like a helicopter propeller blade. Jan thought our tent was trying to kill us.

Using a length of cord, Murray and I managed to tie down the door flap and then, in a crude effort to keep the blowing snow from filling the space, we stacked our packs and equipment against the door. Even so, the tent rattled and shook as if Big Foot himself were pounding on the outside. Confident that the tent would collapse at any moment, sleep was out of the question. Even better— a layer of ice formed on the inner walls of the tent.

We were little more than three cold fish trapped inside of an ice locker. When morning finally came, we were completely exhausted. But we still had ten miles of deep snow to ski across to get out—and every step of the way, the burden of lugging that worthless A-frame tent served as a reminder of the worst night in our collective memories.

And yet, there was something about staring death in its ugly, vacuous face that became a clarifying experience for us. You might say we went to the mountain and returned with an epiphany of sorts. I mean, if the trip had been picture perfect, if the winds had behaved, if our newly designed A-frame tent had done its job, the inspiration for our Trail Dome tent might never have happened.

NECESSITY: THE MOTHER OF INVENTION

The following week at JanSport, we kicked around what happened that frosty night at Blewett Pass. Our love for the winter wilderness, winter camping, and cross-country skiing remained undiminished, but it was painfully clear that we needed a better tent solution. We vowed not to repeat our mistakes and, with the unforgettable experience at Blewett as a guide, we established new design criteria.

Since winter darkness comes early, we knew users would be spending a lot of time inside the shelter. Good, functional, comfortable space was required—we had to incorporate enough room to cook and to change clothes. We also envisioned ourselves sitting in a circle playing cards, drinking beer, or reading a good book after a day of skiing. It struck us then that some sort of uniform shape would maximize the space.

Drawing upon our personal experiences in the field as well as our failed attempt with the traditional tent approach, we brainstormed the idea of shaping a tent to resemble an igloo. While Jan worked on the pattern, we needed some sort of flexible, yet sturdy, pole system to form the dome. When a good friend of

Skip and Murray with a prototype dome tent. Photo by Gail Westin.

mine, Keith Roush from Bozeman, Montana, heard what we were working on, he offered to join us in our quest to perfect the design.

There's nothing like working with people who are passionate about an idea. Between our ideas, hard work, and with varying degrees of success, we ultimately developed and tested three types of lightweight poles: aluminum, solid Fiberglas, and hollow Fiberglas. We started by using what was readily available: fishing pole blanks made of solid Fiberglas. However, we discovered that they would bust under high winds.

We then tried arrow shafts from Easton Aluminum. Easton put some ferrules in for us and we promptly tested those in the field. But, as it turned out, the rods would crack and break where they crimped the ferrule. So that wasn't quite the answer. Thankfully, Easton perfected the hollow aluminium poles including the shock cord technology which has become the standard today.

With the proper poles and fabric pattern, we constructed the first dome tent. Boy, did it attract attention. It was a free-standing thing that looked like an alien space ship. Once assembled, we found that you could pick it up, turn it upside down, and shake it out while retaining its shape. While not exactly a selling feature, the ability to hold the tent with one hand demonstrated the lightweight, yet structural integrity, of the design.

Naturally, before we went public, we tested the dome tent in

83

nearly every weather condition imaginable. Lou Whittaker, among others, got involved by taking the tents up on Mt. Rainier where he found that the sloped sides of our dome held up better in adverse weather—better than an A-frame tent with all that surface area. We also sampled a variety of fabrics and settled on the Dacron used in the exterior walls due to its exceptional strength and its ability to resist the sun's ultraviolet rays better than just about any other material on the market.

A few months after the Blewett Pass epiphany, we were ready to take our new creation to the market. But would the outdoor community get it? After all, most of us grew up with these big Sears cotton, canvas tents—usually in a drab Army green or dark blue fabric. Admittedly, those tents developed holes and were often smelly; putting them up and trying to assemble them in the dark was an absolute nightmare. However, they were the industry standard.

By contrast, we were a couple of hippies trying to peddle a new-fangled, futuristic looking tent in a bright orange or yellow dome shape. Talk about a radical departure from what I had as a kid growing up. Still, our gut told us we had a winner and, refusing to be constrained by tradition, we weren't afraid to try something radical. We just hoped the consumer would catch the vision, too.

We decided to approach Dave Chantler who had traveled with us on that fateful winter ski trip. Dave, who just happened to be the tent buyer at REI, gladly agreed to meet and check out our product. We demonstrated how quickly the Trail Dome tent could be assembled. We explained the tub floor design which would help prevent water from rolling in around the edges. Of special interest was the ability of the dome tent to stand up without the need for staking or guying wires except for extremely high wind conditions. I could sense that we were getting through to him.

At that point, we assured Dave that this, like all JanSport products, had been heavily field-tested and was as rugged as hell. After all, hell is basically what we had to go through to learn how to make the Trail Dome tent.

Maybe Dave felt sorry for us after our prototype A-frame tent attempted to kill us the year before, although I'd like to think he was more of a visionary. Whatever the reality, Dave gave us a shot by buying the first 50 JanSport dome tents for his store. Guess what? They blew out the door without any advertising. Murray, Jan, and I were elated. Dave ordered more, and more, and more.

Within a year, we began taking orders for the Trail Dome tent from across the country. In fact, we were so slammed with orders that we had to sell tents on an allocation basis for many years because we could never make enough. This invention was *the*

85

Skip, Lou, Gombu, and Phrsumba. Photo by Keith Gunnar.

product that put JanSport on the map. Interestingly, the overnight popularity of the Trail Dome tent enabled us to leverage our JanSport pack sales. You know, buy our framepacks and daypacks and we'll provide a supply of dome tents.

Keep in mind that the concept of a dome was not new. In fact, we traced its origins back to pre-Ice Age man. But it was JanSport that introduced this tensioned dome structure to the backpacking community—and since its introduction into the market in 1972, our Dome (with external pole system) has in one form or another been adopted throughout the industry. Come to think of it, the dome tent has practically replaced the A-frame tent for outdoor use.

I'd say that's not bad for a bunch of hippies. But the story doesn't end there.

86

THE BIGGEST MISTAKE OF MY LIFE

In a lot of ways, the dome tent changed people's lives for the better. Whether a serious camper or a weekend hiker, the dome tent provides a more enjoyable experience in the outdoors. For the mountaineer, the dome tent's superior design assured a more suitable shelter and, in many cases, saved lives or allowed a group to continue their climb or expedition. To this day, I carry with me a deep sense of satisfaction knowing that our groovy design forever changed the way the world camps. However, we did make one *slight* mistake.

Okay, it was more like a giant, man-eating blunder.

Are you sitting down?

We never got the dome tent patented.

Here we had with the hottest invention in the industry, and

we failed to patent the product. Of all the details to overlook! Talk about the ultimate disappointment. Frankly, we were more product-driven than we were finance and business driven. We were captivated by the passion of designing something that would change the world; the pursuit of piles of cash really didn't motivate us—okay, maybe a little. Had we gone that extra step to secure the patent, I'd probably be in the Caribbean on a yacht today. There's no question that it was a multi-million dollar idea.

Now, for what it's worth, there were forces operating around us that contributed to this whopper of a blooper. At the time, the K2 Corporation, which manufactured skis, had just purchased JanSport. During the acquisition of JanSport, K2 was in a head-to-head legal battle with the HEAD Ski Company over the construction of a fiberglass ski. Bill Kirschner, one of the founders of K2, had to spend a bunch of money on lawyers to protect their technical design patent.

87

Dome tent used for the 1975 K2 Expedition. Photo by Keith Gunnar.

In the end, K2 won. But Bill was really disenchanted with the experience. And K2 was so consumed by the legal wrangling, they didn't quite know what they had in JanSport. Nor did they really understand what we had with this new "dome tent" product. Rather then spend more money on lawyers to secure a patent, they decided to pass.

At that point, Murray, Jan, and I should have chased the patent on our own. But business was growing. We were working around the clock trying to meet demands as well as making time to further develop and expand our daypack line—not to mention there were some really cool concerts we didn't want to miss. We figured we'd get to it one day. What we didn't know was that after you have a product on the market for a year, if you haven't done anything to protect the patent, you're out of luck.

We went several years before the dome was copied by a competitor. With that, the market changed and everybody decided to jump into making their version of the dome tent.

Stunned, we learned the hard way that we couldn't get a patent, nor could we grandfather the design either. What's the lesson I learned from that experience? It is this: we believed in it, we wanted to do it—we should have just done it. In other words, waiting around for others to do what you *know* ought to be done is never a winning strategy.

Likewise, be thankful when things don't always work out as you originally planned. Often times life's disappointments and detours ultimately open doors to ideas, innovations, and opportunities that would remain otherwise undiscovered. Try looking for a breakthrough the next time you bump into a major roadblock. And, take it from me . . . make sure you secure the patent!

WITH A LITTLE HELP FROM OUR FRIENDS

*W*hat I'm about to say might sound like heresy. All I'm asking is for you to hear me out. Okay? If you've been thinking you must have the latest computer technology, the hottest day planner on the market, a fancy Internet-ready cell phone, a satellite pager, *and* cutting-edge project management and presentation software to succeed in your business, you're in for a surprise. Those "essential business tools" will *not* get you to the top of the corporate ladder.

I'll inch further out on my limb.

I bet if you ditched most of that techno gear today, two things would happen—aside from the fact that your associates would think you're overdue for that head examination. First, you'd discover that you *can* function without these trappings. Secondly, I believe you might just become *more successful* in your job. How can I make such a radical claim?

I'm living proof. Ask those who know me and they'd tell you

that I've never been particularly fond of computers. (I've never owned a Palm Pilot or BlackBerry—although the gurus in our technology department are threatening to get me one.) I'm just now figuring out some of the features on my cell phone. And yet, I've watched our company grow from my uncle's transmission shop in Seattle to what has become an international industry leader. What, then, was the secret to successfully climbing the corporate ladder for me? People.

At the risk of sounding simplistic, success in business boils down to how you meet and treat people. If you will commit to identifying good people, harnessing their energy, and actually following through in the relationships and contacts that you make, you'll find greater success in business than you ever dreamed of.

Far too often, technology gets in the way of the personal touch. I've met these wired business-types, you know, the ones with the space-age headset wrapped around their ear as if they're aboard the *Starship Enterprise*. They'll spend $500 on a Blackberry in order to stay in touch with whomever, and yet they fail to follow-up with the simplest of tasks at hand.

How many times have you heard someone say, "Yeah, I'll get back to you on that," or, "I'll get you hooked up with someone from our warranty department," or, "I'm going to send you a catalogue as soon as I get back to my office," or maybe "I'll email that info ASAP." What happens? More often than not, *nothing* happens. They drop the ball. And forget about going the extra distance by remembering someone's name, or birthday, their unique skills, or perhaps what's going on in their family life. While people are hungry to be treated with care and respect and that little extra personal touch, few make it happen. In fact, it is the exceptional business person who does this consistently.

Using little more than the low-tech instruments of a 3x5 card and a pen, I've made a habit over the years of jotting down notes as I speak with an employee or someone I meet in the field. If I've promised them something, I write it down. If I notice that they might benefit from a JanSport resource, I make a note of it. If they have a special skill or need, I'll record that and actually make a connection for them with the right department.

Granted, technology can help with this task and I'm not suggesting that its usage is necessarily a bad thing. But technology is not a replacement for common sense or common courtesy. Nor can it mask a lack of authenticity as we relate to others. It's one thing to say you care about fellow employees, associates, or key contacts. It's another thing to demonstrate that care with action and follow through.

Speaking of treating others with a spirit of authentic care, maybe there was something to the Sixties love-your-neighbor movement after all. Remember the Youngbloods? They sang, "Come on people now / smile on your brother. / Everybody get together, try to love one another / right now." Let me illustrate how this caring, friend-raising approach can produce fruit for your business.

WALK A MILE IN MY SHOES

The early Seventies for JanSport was marked by a steady growth of our product line. With the invention of our dome tent in 1972 and the huge success it produced, our mailbag became stuffed with letters from across the country from people who had caught wind about the "hippie tent" and wanted to know where they could buy one. Others thanked us for introducing such a practical piece of outdoor gear. Of course, there were the retailers outside of our distribution channels who wanted to start carrying JanSport products. Occasionally you'd get a guy peddling a new idea or someone looking for a job.

I remember sifting through the mailbag one day when an envelope with two little Vibram footprints stamped on the outside caught my eye. Vibram was a manufacturer of outdoor footwear who also provided rugged terrain soles to retrofit boots for hikers. Looking at the return address I noticed it was from a Peter Jenkins in New Orleans.

I didn't know Peter, but I was fascinated by the way he had taken the Vibram logo of two footprints and affixed them to the letter. That got my attention. In spite of how busy we were, something in my gut nudged me to call him. Who would have thought that answering a random piece of mail would lead to a life-long friendship? A bit surprised, yet thankful for my call, Peter told me his story.

Briefly, Peter grew up in Greenwich, Connecticut. As a highly motivated person, he worked hard to go to college and get his degree. And yet, during the course of his studies, he became disenchanted with America. Like many students of his generation, two key issues fueled this disillusion: the Vietnam War and President Richard Nixon's Watergate mess. Aware of Peter's unrest, a janitor at his college suggested that before he totally blew off America, maybe he ought to take a good look at it first.

Peter accepted that challenge and, upon graduation, came up with the novel idea to walk across America to see for himself what his country had to offer. But before embarking on the journey, he stopped at the offices of National Geographic. Without an appointment, Peter just walked in and told them he planned to walk from upper New York, head down through the Deep South and then make his way west until he reached the Oregon coast.

Peter explained that he'd be traveling with his dog, Cooper, a half-Alaskan Malamute and a backpack with a handful of personal belongings. He asked if the magazine would be interested in his story. They were interested and offered some modest support by supplying an Alpine Designs frame pack and an A-frame tent. In the fall of 1973, Peter set off on an adventure that would change his life, and mine, as it turned out.

By the time Peter reached New Orleans, he noticed that his gear was falling apart. There was no way he could make the rest of the trek using the pack and tent that he set out with. At that

point, he remembered two things: thumbing through a JanSport catalogue back in college and visiting an outdoor store that carried our products. Peter, an art major, found our catalogues fascinating, primarily because they were so different from those produced by other outdoor companies. He decided to send me a letter explaining his goal.

Peter and Barbara Jenkins on their Walk Across America.

At the end of our conversation, he told me he needed a really good frame pack as well as a tent as he continued his walk across America. I liked his story and the passion that drove him to explore America on foot. Frankly, I had never heard of anybody going to that extreme and so I told him we'd send him the JanSport D-3 frame pack and the JanSport Trail Dome tent. Rather than make a false promise just to sound good or to string him along, I followed up immediately.

Peter called from time to time to keep me posted about his travels. He would finance his walk by taking jobs in some of the towns he passed through. When he had enough money to buy the supplies he needed, he would continue on his journey. While he was in New Orleans, he met a young lady named Barbara, fell in love, and got married. When Peter left New Orleans to continue his walk, Barbara went with him.

Several months later as winter arrived, he called with another request. His sister Winky would be joining them for a portion of the journey in Utah and needed a pack—could we help? I was just thrilled to see Peter's passion and commitment to doing what seemed impossible. If the company of his sister helped him reach his goal, so be it. We promptly arranged a frame pack for her, too. Incidentally, I learned that while Winky was walking along the road, she got hit from behind by a car. She was thrown into a ditch—and survived. The police on the scene determined that she was saved by the JanSport frame she had on her back.

About five years after taking the first step on this amazing journey, Peter and Barbara reached the Oregon coast. I knew from our conversations that National Geographic would be hosting a big event upon his arrival. Murray and I were invited to join the celebration. Of course, we were pleased that our gear held up for Peter under such constant use. When we arrived, about three hundred people were on hand, including a host of media and photographers. That night, we met Peter and his entire family for the first time. Finally, I had a face to put with his name after several years of conversation. We really hit it off.

Several months later, in 1979, we got together again for the release of his book, *A Walk Across America* which became a *New York Times* best-seller. It also sold more than four million copies, an almost unheard of feat for a first-time author. As Peter described his journey in the book, he mentioned the products he used in a very non-commercial way—including those we supplied from JanSport. Interestingly, his passing comments helped us reach a broader market than just the small outdoor community.

Long after the lights and cameras moved on from focusing on that book, Peter and I continued to travel together and grow as friends.

Looking back on my forty years at JanSport, I can honestly say one of my key abilities is that I can assess opportunities and recognize those which will be a good investment for us; I can tell which are most compatible with what we stand for. Peter and his trek was definitely one of those jewels. He has been—and continues to be—an ambassador for JanSport in an authentic way. Without question, JanSport has benefited from our association with Peter, which started because I paid a little attention to that letter from him many years ago. I followed through with my promises, and I invested in the friendship. That's what harnessing the power of people is all about. It's a win-win deal.

While I managed to practice what I preach about friend raising with Peter, there was also a time when I blew it big time.

95

YES, WE HAVE NO BANANAS

In 1979, Bob Shaw, Craig Perpich, and I traveled from our headquarters in Seattle to New York City to attend a college bookstore trade show. Bob and Craig were on our sales team. Believe it or not, we flew the 3,000 miles without the added enticement of a cool concert in the New York area motivating us to head east. I just knew the event was a big deal and that our competition would be there representing their gear to the college bookstore buyers.

As you might expect, most of the manufacturers hoped to generate sales and develop their customer base. We were there, however, on a reconnaissance mission. We wanted to understand the workings of that particular trade show and viewed it as a growth opportunity for future expansion down the road. If the truth were known, we didn't have enough production capacity at that time to service any new customers.

As we walked the trade room floor, we were approached by Rick Becker, a young sales representative. Rick loved our brand and lobbied us hard to become a sales rep of JanSport to the college bookstore market—an area where I knew we could use some help. Wanting to show us just how connected he was on the campus scene, he introduced us to one of his customers, Paul Delorey. Paul was a likeable fellow with an exceptional spirit who managed the bookstore at Eastern Michigan University.

For the better part of an hour, we talked about packs and products and bookstores and everything related to the college market. I could tell that Paul had a great personality, solid instincts, a strong commitment to properly servicing the student market, and

96

a playful sense of humor. No wonder I really liked him right off of the bat. But that's when things hit a snag.

When we were done talking about JanSport, Paul wanted to place an order for his store right on the spot. I had to tell him thanks, but no thanks. A puzzled look crossed his face as if he thought I was kidding around. After all, this *was* a sales convention and JanSport was in the business of selling packs, right? Although that was true, I assured him we couldn't sell him any packs because we didn't have the capacity to add new accounts. I wasn't rude, I was just stating the facts.

Given my ability to identify good people and great opportunities in the past, you would have thought that I might have found a way to make things work for Paul. But for reasons I still don't know, I didn't nurture the relationship with Paul as I had done with Peter Jenkins. How was I to know that the guy I just turned down would one day become my boss?

Several years later, unknown to me, Paul was hired away from the Eastern Michigan bookstore to work for a company called Downers. Evidently, company president Dan Spalding saw the same spark in Paul that I had noticed—with one difference. Dan asked Paul to come to work for him. At that point, the plot thickened. Downers purchased JanSport in 1982 from our parent company K2 and Dan needed someone to expand the college bookstore sales effort. He picked Paul Delorey.

Paul Delorey, president of JanSport from 1986 to 2000.

One of Paul's first assignments was to hop on a plane and check out our Everett operation. With a firm knock on my door, Paul stepped into my office. He had this playful, ear-to-ear grin on his face. His face looked familiar, but I hadn't seen him in years, not since that brief hour-long meeting. He extended his hand and, with a firm, confident grip, he said, "Hello, Skip. Remember me? I'm the guy in New York that you said couldn't buy any JanSport packs!" I was floored. While we had a good laugh over that bit of irony, I couldn't help but wonder how I missed cultivating that relationship.

In the months ahead, Paul immersed himself in the JanSport philosophy of doing business, our love for the outdoors, the Mt. Rainier climbs, and especially the core value that we add fun to everything we do. He was an amazingly fast study who easily captured the spirit of our mission. As one of the co-founders, I spent a significant amount of time with him sharing our history and goals.

It didn't take long for Paul to distinguish himself within the ranks of the company. A master at cultivating and caring for people on the team, Paul was promoted to be the President of JanSport where he served in that role from 1986 until 2001. During his tenure, Paul even taught me a thing or two about harnessing people power. After all, there's nothing like a little help from your friends to get you to the top.

ONE YAK
BACKED

On the surface, it sounded like a cool idea. In reality, our great concept almost got us killed. Isn't this starting to sound familiar?

You see, my friend and business consultant Dan McConnell and I had spent an afternoon brainstorming ways to help fund the 1982 China-Everest expedition on behalf of Lou Whittaker and the American team of climbers. Whether assaulting the North Face of Everest or tackling Mt. Kangchenjunga, one of the most difficult parts of any climb is financing the expedition—in this case with upwards of $200,000.

We knew we could assemble the best group of climbers, supplies, and gear, but without the proper funding all we'd have is a pipe dream. Dan and I got to work. First and foremost, we knew there was no way we would tackle this funding goal with a traditional bake sale, car wash, or raffle. We wanted something memorable and something *fun*.

In keeping with our quirky, nothing-is-too-crazy mindset, we came up with this radical idea to sell a photo of a yak. After all, yaks traditionally play a key role in any successful climb in that region. For the China-Everest climb, these ox-like beasts would be used to lug five tons of gear and propane from base camp to the advanced base camp—a difficult journey ascending almost 2,000 feet of frozen tundra. In that remote corner of the world, a yak was better than a Hummer.

Besides, the burly, wild Tibetan Yak and the American hippie are similar creatures—both are on the endangered species list. Just as the hippie wears beads, flowers, and bell-bottoms, yaks are frequently festooned with beads, feathers, and bells around their necks. Both have long, shaggy hair. Neither find bathing a high priority, and both prefer being high—that is, the yak thrives in high altitudes while the hippie seeks either a natural high or, as is sometimes the case, a chemically-assisted high.

While I can't say for sure, I suspect there might have been some level of divine irony at play back then. During the Summer of Love, the hippie's car of choice was an air-cooled, 1967 Volkswagen Bug—which, at 1,786 pounds, just happens to weigh *precisely* what the average yak weighed after an evening of grazing and a stomach full of digested snow. Plus, the concept of selling a yak to raise funds was consistent with the fourth principle we live by at JanSport. Namely, *we make fun a part of everything that we do.* Selling yak sponsorships seemed like a perfect fit.

Dan and I decided to offer small businesses in the Seattle area a deal whereby they would get a framed and mounted photo of their yak on Mt. Everest along with their business name by the yak. Best of all, their plaque would be signed by each of the expe-

A Yak Plaque for the One Yak Backed promotion. Photo by Dan McConnell.

dition team members—something these store owners could proudly hang in the entry way to their business.

The Official Back-A-Yak program was born. We sold yak sponsorships for $327. Frankly, we settled on that odd dollar amount just to be odd; it was also an amount we figured that a mom and pop business would find affordable. To sweeten the deal, we set up a not-for-profit corporation so that the contributions would be tax deductible. Now that we had our great idea, we needed to brainstorm how we'd pull it off.

Clearly, there were no catalog companies specializing in "Yak Plaques." So, relying upon our own imaginations, we figured we could get a Sherpa to let us stand next to his yak holding a large blank, white card for the shot. With those pictures in hand, we'd come back to the office, make fifty or a hundred duplicates as needed, and then write the name of each business on the blank, white card. Remember, this was long before the day of Photoshop. We would then place that photo into a plastic frame along with the China-Everest 1982 logo and the personal signatures.

We decided to take the photos of the yaks at base camp on Mt. Everest—not that we had any experience staging a photo shoot at 16,900 feet with a beast of burden who hadn't consented to doing pictures when he was enlisted for the expedition. If the yak gave us any flack, we assumed his Sherpa would coax the yak into being a good sport.

Unfortunately, we didn't factor in the language barrier. We spoke English. The Sherpa spoke a dialect of Tibetan that sounded to us much like a cross between any number of cartoon characters and the Klingons from *Star Trek*. In hindsight, even with an interpreter, our communication was bound to hit a few snags. Sometimes ignorance in business is bliss.

YAKETY YAK

While we were convinced the Back-A-Yak promotion was a winner, we still had to take to the streets of Seattle and actually sell the idea. But where to start? Keep in mind, I had no formal training in marketing strategies, donor relations, or even entry level door-to-door sales techniques. Somehow it just made sense to begin with the best leads that were right under our noses: the retailers we regularly supplied with JanSport gear. They became our A-list.

Since these outlets were outdoor retailers and climbing shops, we believed they would most likely catch the vision: if they'd back a yak, they would help an American team be the first to scale the Great Couloirs of the North Face of Everest. I imagine most marketing textbooks would call this selling to your "affinity group."

Two yaks on Everest.

After exhausting the A-List, we planned to target the neighborhoods where several of the climbers lived, calling on the barber shops, bakeries, and other local businesses. Again, this just seemed logical since there's something very American about supporting the home team.

Granted, most of the store owners we approached had about as much use for a yak as they would a kayak. Still, we had to try.

I remember going into a bakery with Dan. He figured that rather than wasting time engaging in small talk, it was better to go with the direct approach. Dan cut to the chase:

"Hi, I'm selling yaks."

The guy looked at us funny—he sort of had this puckered face look as if he had bitten down on a piece of garlic. Being a good sport, he grunted, "Uh-huh. How much are they?"

"They're $327 dollars," Dan said with a steady smile.

"Right. And why do I need a yak?" He scratched the back of his head. "Fellows, this is a bakery, not a butcher shop."

Unfazed, Dan launched into the prepared speech about Lou Whittaker's expedition and the need for yaks to make the trip. As the owner straightened out the trays of donuts, I chimed in that he'd be playing a key role in shaping history and that many of the climbers were his neighbors. After several minutes of making the pitch, the baker, clearly frustrated, held up a hand and said, "But what am I going to *do* with this thing?"

Come to think of it, I'm not sure we made it clear that we were not going to actually deliver a live yak to his doorstep. Dan, sensing we were about to lose a sale, walked over to the wall where the baker had a bunch of posters taped. Dan said, "Instead of these posters, you're going to get a photograph of a yak with your store's name on it. It's going to say, 'Joe's Bakery.' It will be *your* yak. You'll be helping a bunch of guys from Seattle go to the top of the world. Now, isn't that about the neatest thing you've ever heard?"

For a long moment, the baker studied Dan and then me. He said, "Look, I'm not sure that going to the top of the world is the neatest thing I've heard, but yaks sound kinda cool. I think I'll buy one." He wrote a check out on the spot. While that didn't happen often—more frequently we'd be shown the door—it was a happy day. By the end of the fund raising push, we had sold about 100 yaks and made almost $40,000 from the Back-A-Yak promotion. That, coupled with several larger corporate sponsorships, enabled us to meet our funding goals. Now we had to actually deliver on the promised yaks. That's where the story gets dicey.

YAK ATTACK

Fast forward several months. Upon arriving at the Everest base camp, Dan and I knew one of our prime duties was to return home with the official yak photograph. We had been working on the various last minute preparations at base camp for about a week when we noticed the herd of yaks making their way through the valley below. The bells, suspended from their necks, announced their presence long before we could see the entire yak procession.

With the sun hanging low in the sky, we saw about fifty yaks festooned in colorful headdresses following the lead of their Sherpas. As the entourage approached us, it was a real sight to behold—and *smell*. You might say their arrival was sort of a multi-media experience. No joke, a pack of yaks would cause a skunk to hold his breath.

Not wanting to miss an opportunity to get our shot, Dan said, "Skip, let's get our picture right now." We knew the next morning they'd be headed up the mountain to the advanced base camp. It was entirely possible that the Sherpa might want to get an early start. If so, they'd be gone and we'd miss our photo shoot. Dan and I went over with an interpreter to talk to the keepers of the yaks. We quickly told them what we wanted to accomplish, which, on the surface, seemed simple enough. I mean, how difficult could it be to stand next to a yak while holding a little white cardboard for a photo?

Our request was being translated to the first herdsman as Dan ventured forward to stand next to the closest yak. Without warning, the yak started to freak out—I'm talking all 1,800 pounds of yak hair and stink went flailing around with about as much force as a localized tornado. The yak bucked and stomped and snorted as Dan desperately tried to get out of the way. One swift kick and he could forget about the expedition.

Thankfully, Dan managed to get out of harm's way. With a sweep of his hand, he said, "Be my guest, Skipper. Maybe you know a better way." I figured what harm could there be in trying, right? I took the white card and headed toward the Sherpa of a

105

different yak. I didn't get within ten feet when the yak went nuts. I mean, that yak chased me around base camp as if I had insulted his mother. I never ran so fast in my life.

On hindsight, we probably should have given more careful consideration to the timing of our photo shoot. It was the end of the day and the yaks were hacked. They had just lumbered their way across rough terrain all day and were worn out. Now some silly white boys were trying to get them to pose for a picture. The yaks were probably thinking, *No way, man. You must be crazy.*

The sun was dropping like a rock. Our window of opportunity was about to slam shut and we knew it. Admittedly, after two close calls, tossing in the towel seemed consistent with the idea of living to see another day. But we knew if we didn't get the photo and deliver on the Back-A-Yak program, there would be a hundred store owners forming a posse to find those two long-hairs who took their money for a bogus scam.

Dan had another idea. We would just give the white card to the yak herdsman and have *him* stand next to his wild beast. He did and the yak didn't flip out this time. Dan quickly snapped as many pictures as possible in hopes of capturing at least something we could work with. Thankfully, we ended up getting shots with three or four different yaks and their Sherpas before we lost daylight.

Later, back at the JanSport shop, we developed the photos, assembled the plaques, and proudly presented them to the store owners. Universally, the reaction was the same: Everyone thought it was a pretty cool deal. In fact, the promotion was so well received, we did it again two years later for the 1984 China-Everest expedition with even greater success.

THE SCHOOL OF YAK

I'm sure there's a business principle somewhere in that experience. Sometimes the only way to reach a goal is to take yourself out of the picture. I realize that may sound counterintuitive. After all, it's been my observation that most business men and women who seek to move up the corporate ladder tend to think that they've always got to be front and center. You know, never share the credit or the glory. However, when I fight that natural it's-all-about-me tendency by allowing others to step into the spotlight, I ultimately advance and reach my personal goals in ways I hadn't anticipated.

Here's a second business principle: show appreciation to those who help you succeed at your goals. Again, that may seem obvious. Unfortunately, in the dog-eat-dog push to reach the top of the corporate pack, extending a kind word of thanks to those who

Tibetan Yak drivers viewing a polaroid. Photo by 1984 team.

helped you along the way is a rare gift. Most of the time, saying thanks costs us next to nothing. Whether it's an email, a note card sent through snail mail, or a phone call, an attitude of sincere gratitude creates an environment of goodwill.

However, I'll be the first to admit that sometimes exhibiting gratitude comes with a price. Case in point. After the Sherpa helped us get a series of photos with their yaks, they invited us to sit down and drink yak butter tea—sort of like a ceremony of friendship. To have declined them would have been a serious insult. To accept their offer for tea would validate and thank them for their participation in our project.

So what's the big deal about having tea?

You wouldn't be wondering that if you'd ever tasted yak butter tea. Basically, the Sherpa carry pouches attached to their belts filled with butter made from yaks' milk. As you might imagine, without refrigeration, most yak butter is rancid. At tea time, they boil a pot of water and then reach into their flask for a glob of the yak yuck. This goop gets lumped into a cup along with the tea leaves and whatever else they fancy at the moment.

As Westerners, the immediate reaction would be to skim the yak butter off of the top of the cup—not that it would help matters much. But it would have been extremely rude, since a thick head of yak butter is the way the locals enjoy tea. Dan and I just had to smile, suck it up and then hope we could find a beer fast enough to wash it down.

Of course, there is something *worse* than hot yak butter tea. Try drinking it solidified and COLD!

HIPPIES ON EVEREST: WE'RE NOT IN KANSAS ANYMORE

There are peaks in the world that are steeper than the majestic profile of Mt. Everest. A number of mountains are harder or more technically difficult to scale, such as K2. And yet, an attempt on Mt. Everest never fails to capture the imagination of the seasoned climber as well as the part-time novice. As a member of the 1984 China-Everest Expedition, our quest to successfully summit that graceful yet powerful giant was an unparalleled adventure for me.

You've got to go back to my childhood to appreciate the dynamic here. I was a Kansas-born-and-bred hippie who lived, trekked, and played in the prairie. There are no real mountains in Kansas. There *is* Mt. Sunflower which sits just a mile from the border of Colorado, but with an elevation of just 4,039 feet, I'd say it qualifies as a "mountain wannabe." For the most part, I grew up completely unacquainted with the realties of standing in the shadow of a true alpine peak.

Imagine then what it felt like to gaze upon the mother of all mountains, Everest, whose perpetually snow-covered peak slices the sky at 29,028 feet above sea level. Words simply fail to do justice to this gem of the Himalayas.

Whether or not you're from Kansas, to stand on the highest point on the planet is every climber's four-minute mile, every mountaineer's walk in outer space, every alpinist's impossible dream. For those who have taken life's path into the mountains, to scale Everest is the pinnacle experience of a lifetime. Which is why I was caught completely off guard when Lou Whittaker invited this Kansas boy to join him on what became the first American team to summit Everest on the North Couloir Route, which is accessible through China and Tibet.

Lou and I were sitting outside the Camp Muir guide hut, located at the 10,000 foot elevation mark on Mt. Rainier, discussing his upcoming Mt. Everest climb. It was late June, 1983, and we had just finished a beautiful day involved in training thirty-five people from all over the United States on glacier travel and other ice climbing techniques during one of our JanSport dealer climbs. Looking across the valley at Mt. Adams from our perch, we shared a deep sense of gratification from our work with the enthusiastic group of participants.

Lou, in his usual soft-spoken way, turned and asked me if I'd like to go to Mt. Everest with him and the climbing team in 1984. My reaction was one of total disbelief. I had fantasized for years on seeing the Himalayas or being on an expedition of that magnitude. But being only a weekend mountaineer and backpacker, the reality of it seemed very far away. When I realized Lou was as serious as an avalanche, I answered without hesitation, "You bet!"

Lou had personally selected a top-notch team of climbers, all varying in experience, abilities, and motivation. Upon our return from Mt. Rainier, we started to meet as a team once a month. Each member focused on their area of responsibility. I quickly came to see that the details of preparing for a major expedition are endless. My area of expertise was to work with Phil Ershler and Greg Wilson, an RMI guide, on equipment development. Phil, also a full-time RMI guide, had many years of expedition experience. This was to be Phil's third trip to Everest in as many years, while it would be Greg Wilson's first major expedition.

The concepts of expedition equipment development—durability, light weight, and function—are the same for the everyday backpacker, camper, or traveler. The challenge for us was to assemble the very best possible gear. I knew that the success of the entire expedition could depend on the quality and condition of the equipment. I also knew the most reliable form of testing is actual

111

Mt. Rainier dealer climb. Photo by Keith Gunnar.

use, and that testing of the expedition equipment would ultimately benefit our JanSport line of gear. We made sure that each bartack, each snap, and each fabrication was the state of the art. As soon as our prototypes were available, various team members made test runs on the new equipment during their training climbs.

For the two months before we left, my mind was preoccupied with preparations for this mammoth challenge. I contemplated how my life might be changed by Everest and what it would be like to meet new people and experience new cultures on the other side of the world. I relished the thought of testing my own abilities on Chomolungma—that's the name the Chinese gave Everest. Loosely translated, it means "Mother Goddess of the Earth." I knew I would have to push myself as part of the support team setting up base camp.

I also had another idea: *Wouldn't it be great if we had a writer traveling with us? Maybe he could do a book on the story.* I shared this idea with Lou who agreed that it was a very cool concept. I decided to call my friend and author, Peter Jenkins, to see if he'd join us and perhaps chronicle some of the story. I told him that Lou had put this trip together and that we'd travel to Tibet and become some of the first westerners in a long time to enter Lhasa, the capital. Sure enough, Peter jumped at the chance. I was grateful for his companionship. His wild, fun-loving spirit was energizing.

We also made arrangements for a PBS camera crew to catch the expedition on film. Sponsored in part by Dan Spalding and Kim VanderHyden, the owners of JanSport at the time, the PBS crew came and filmed the *Winds of Everest*. Narrated by John Denver, the *Winds of Everest* aired on PBS for many years to come and captured the heart and soul, the ups and downs, and the thrills and chills of our odyssey. Incidentally, upon our return, Peter penned *Across China*, a book that landed on the *New York Times* bestseller list for three months.

But I'm getting ahead of the story.

PLANES, TRAINS, AND A GREYHOUND BUS

Before I knew it, the preparations were complete, the funds were raised, and our airplane was heading due West. As the plane cut a path through the clouds, a host of thoughts filled my mind. I was struck by the fact that, in some way, all of my life had been a preparation for this trip. Come to think of it, my mom had been training me early on to travel and to have confidence in unfamiliar surroundings; she must have had a hunch that both would ultimately become a big part of my life.

When I was just five years old, for example, mom put me on a Greyhound bus from Russell, Kansas to Grainfield to go to my grandmother's house—all alone. She told the bus driver that I was getting off in Grainfield and that my grandmother would be waiting there on the other end. You could do that with little fear in those days.

In my young mind, that trip was such a giant adventure. Just as I was now anticipating what awaited us on Mt. Everest, there was a lot of anticipation at that age over what might

Skip with catfish.

happen around the next bend in the road. I sat in the front of the bus with my little heart rattling away at the thrill of it all. That would be the first of many such jaunts.

At age twelve, having spent the summer fishing and hiking with my cousin Murray in Seattle, I needed to get home to Great Bend. It was decided that I'd take the train by myself from Seattle to Portland and then on to Russell. Having said an emotionally-charged goodbye to my aunt and cousins, I boarded the train in the afternoon and arrived in Portland that evening.

A blast of hot air released from the brakes served as an announcement that we had parked. I grabbed my pack and headed into the station. I wandered around a maze of trains that, while stationed, still pumped plumes of grey smoke skyward. The smell of grease and oil hung in the air and the dimly lit train platforms were littered with ticket stubs. I could see the steam rising off of the tracks, but I was having trouble identifying which train was my train.

I approached a conductor and told him that I need to get on the train to Russell, Kansas. He looked me over as if I were Fagin, the child pickpocket from *Oliver Twist*. I'm sure he was wondering what a boy so young was doing traveling alone. After a long moment, he scratched his head and directed me to the correct train. About three days after leaving Seattle, sleeping in my upright seat as needed, I arrived in Kansas. That was the start of my first adventure travel.

Whether fishing for the first time at age four with grasshoppers for bait, or pheasant hunting at age ten at Cheyenne Bottoms—a big flyaway for ducks and geese—my folks instilled in me a thirst for adventure and a knack for problem solving. I had

114

Mt. Rainier (Photo by Keith Gunnar)

Below: Lou Whittaker climbing a serac on Mt. Rainier. (Photo by Keith Gunnar)

Above: Lou Whittaker on Mt. Rainier. (Photo by Keith Gunnar)

A store in Katmandu, Nepal.
(Photo by Skip Yowell)

Above: Skip Yowell and
Peter Jenkins at the
Everest base camp in Tibet.
(Photo by Russ Cole)

Above: Lou Whittaker,
Skip Yowell, and Nawang
Gombu at HMI camp at
17,000 feet. (Photo by
Winnie Kingsbury)

Above: A friendly yak on the
Kangchenjunga expedition.
Left: Great Wall of China
photo by Skip Yowell.
(Photos by Skip Yowell)

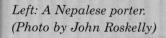
Left: A Nepalese porter.
(Photo by John Roskelly)

Above: Porters on the
Kangchenjunga expedition.
(Photo by Skip Yowell)

Tibetan children.
(Photo by Dave Mahre)

A village in Nepal.
(Photo by Skip Yowell)

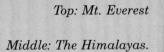

Top: Mt. Everest

Middle: The Himalayas.

Bottom: Porters at
the Kangchenjunga
base camp.
(Photos by Skip Yowell)

On Kangchenjunga
between Camp 2 and
Camp 3. (Photo by
George Dunn)

Left: Nawang Gombu,
Lou Whittaker, and
Skip Yowell on
Kangchenjunga.
(Photo by Preston
Spencer)

Top: Potala Palace in Lhasa, Tibet.

Middle Left: Bhutan festival dance.

Right: Trees in Bhutan (Photos by Skip Yowell)

Above: A decorated door in Bhutan.

*Right: Mike Cisler on
Mt. Cook, New Zealand.*

*Below: A view from
the Milford Trek in
New Zealand.*

*Santorini
Greek Islands
(Photos by
Skip Yowell)*

Custer State Park, SD.
(Photo by Skip Yowell)

Middle: Looking toward Mt. Adams. (Photo by Peter Whittaker)
Bottom: North Cascades (Photo by Skip Yowell)

A store in Kenya, Africa. (Photo by Skip Yowell)

Above: Mt. Kilimanjaro, Africa. (Photo by Skip Yowell)

Left: Skip Yowell during a trip to Mombassa. (Photo by Ingrid Whittaker)

Top: Arches National Park in Utah.

Middle: Jan Lewis in New Mexico.

Bottom: Skip's sunflower field. (Photos by Skip Yowell)

1st prototype travel pack, 1974.

Top: Skip Yowell with an early dome tent.

Middle: Skip and Murray with camping gear.

Bottom: Phrsumba, Jan, Gombu; second row: Murray and Skip for a catalog cover photo shoot. (Photos by Marsha Burns)

Right: Kangchenjunga team poster, 1989.

Middle: Big City Mountaineers trip to Holy Cross, CO. (Photo by Keith Roush)

Bottom: Big City Mountaineers trip. (Photo by Keith Roush)

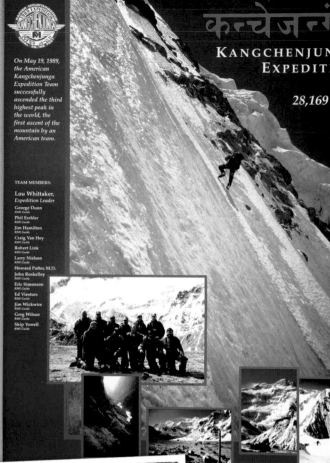

कन्चेजन्गा

KANGCHENJUNGA EXPEDITION

28,169 Feet

On May 19, 1989, the American Kangchenjunga Expedition Team successfully ascended the third highest peak in the world, the first ascent of the mountain by an American team.

TEAM MEMBERS:

Lou Whittaker,
Expedition Leader
George Dunn
RMI Guide
Phil Ershler
RMI Guide
Jim Hamilton
RMI Guide
Craig Van Hoy
RMI Guide
Robert Link
RMI Guide
Larry Nielson
RMI Guide
Howard Putter, M.D.
RMI Guide
John Roskelley
RMI Guide
Eric Simonson
RMI Guide
Ed Viesturs
RMI Guide
Jim Wickwire
RMI Guide
Greg Wilson
RMI Guide
Skip Yowell
RMI Guide

CORDURA nylon

JANSPORT
QUALITY OUTDOOR GEAR

Celebrating 30 years of innovation, adventure, and general outdoor grooviness.

40th anniversary pack label of Skip's popcorn.

30th anniversary poster. Artwork by Elgin / Syferd.

Below: Skip and Paul Delorey for JanSport's "Bring Your Dog to Work" day. (Photo by Peggy McNally)

1st Shake 'N' Bake t-shirt with sponsor logos.

Previous Page: JanSport collage by Lee Fenyves and Kelly Dwyer.

Top: Winnie and Skip in Bhutan. (Photo by Penny Legate)

Middle: Quinn Yowell. (Photo by Skip Yowell)

Bottom: Skip and Quinn in Maui. (Photo by Penny Lutz)

a hunch that those informal life lessons as a youth would serve me well on Mt. Everest. Was I really ready? Time would tell.

Expectant as children on Christmas morning, we landed in Lhasa, the capital of Tibet. The clearest sign that we had traveled back in time was the home of the famous Dalai Lama, god-king of Tibet built in the Seventh Century A.D. Called the Potala Palace, this near pyramid-sized royal residence was nestled in the foothills of Marpo Ri, also known as the Red Mountain. With inward-sloping exterior walls, the breathtaking fortress-like palace sports more than 1,000 rooms. Potala's many gold-plated roofs pierced the pristine sky with intermittent bursts of golden reflection. How they managed to build that massive structure at 12,000 feet above sea level without the aid of modern construction equipment is beyond me.

The next day we strolled through the Lhasa market. The friendly and happy Tibetans crowded around us, totally fascinated by these strangers with hair on their arms and legs. You see, for the most part, Tibetans do not have body hair. It was funny to see the villagers pulling at my blonde hair to see if it was real. And, at one point, as I often do, I removed my shirt to soak up the sun. That prompted a swarm of Tibetans to crowd around and pull at my chest hair—I can't say that's ever happened to me before.

EAT OR DIE

Believe it or not, food was a major topic of conversation and concern. Team members knew it was absolutely important to maintain their body weight if they were to stay healthy and strong on the mountain. On a typical climb, the body needs upwards of

115

6,000 calories a day to maintain body mass. The problem is that at the higher altitudes, the body doesn't absorb nutrition efficiently, making weight loss an unwanted byproduct of the climb. Climbers do best when they at least start at the proper weight.

Our Chinese cooks made that goal very difficult by serving us a diet of yak, dog, pigeon, unbaked dough and carp—and that was the stuff we actually recognized. During one of our last dinners in Lhasa, for instance, Peter Jenkins reached into his stew and pulled out the head of a chicken with the comb still on it. Holding it up as if it were toxic, Peter said, "Hey, anybody want this?" One of our Chinese interpreters grabbed it right out of his chopsticks and ate it whole. Lunch at KFC never prepared me for that exchange.

As we headed from Lhasa farther inland toward the Everest base camp, we stayed at several of the villages along the way for a couple of days. We needed that time to work on our logistics, to acclimatize, and to get ready for our trek up the mountain.

While walking to breakfast one morning, we noticed that five or six little puppies were playing near the kitchen door. The next morning on the way to breakfast, we noticed there were only three puppies. That struck us as odd until we found out that the puppies were cooked as food—which for me brought new meaning to the word hotdog. In some of the places where we ate, we could actually see rats running around in the kitchen and knew they'd end up on our plates as a local delicacy.

On more than one occasion, team member Dan McConnell would push his plate away, unwilling to feast on rat meat. Watching Dan do this time and time again, I had to wonder how the big guy was surviving, but I later learned that Dan had a whole duffel bag of canned hams that he was eating on the side. I knew his duffel was too big.

Other than the veteran 1982 team members who had learned from their previous trip to bring their own food, most of us lost a considerable amount of weight on the "Tibetan Diet Plan" by the time we reached base camp.

At least we didn't burn unnecessary calories lugging our gear, thanks to the caravan of thirty-three yaks we obtained. Each yak carried 110 pounds of supplies from base camp to Camp 1, saving over a month of ferrying loads. Because the yaks could travel where horses wouldn't, they greatly contributed to the expedition's success. This was especially true considering that no porters or Sherpas were used on this seldom-climbed, Tibetan side of Mt. Everest.

Each day brought a new and fascinating experience. For example, Pete Whittaker, George Dunn, Phil Ershler, and John Smolich were looking for a site to establish Camp 5 at 25,000 feet when they noticed a small mound with a piece of ripstop showing. After chipping away snow and ice with their ice axes, a JanSport label appeared. It was a China-Everest tent left by the Ultima Thule expedition after their unsuccessful attempt that spring. The tent had survived the monsoon season. It was quickly dug out, named the Ice Palace, and used for over a month at the higher camps, withstanding persistent 100 mile per hour winds.

Another time, a sleeping bag, tied to an oxygen bottle and left outside for a week, would later provide warmth for Phil Ershler in a snow cave bivouac. The bag with Qualofil insulation and Entrant fabric lived up to its reputation. Two months of living in the snow at high altitudes allowed no margin for error in gear or action. I was thankful that we did our homework by bringing only JanSport gear that had been thoroughly field tested.

I should point out that not everyone who is a part of an expedition is assigned to climb the summit. For instance, my duties were with the support team members at base camp. When our work was done, we prepared to descend from camp. I, however, felt an overwhelming urge to join Lou and the others on the assault team. It was as if the peak were beckoning me to scale its icy shoulders. I didn't want to leave—at least not yet. In that moment, I came to understand a little more of what compelled the other climbers to endure the hardships which lay in front of them as they headed to the top of the world . . . and man, were they in for a life and death drama.

LIFE ON THE EDGE

Working as a team, our climbers built a logistical pyramid, ferrying loads to ever higher camps. These sanctuaries provided a place to rest and gave shelter from the brutal conditions. Above 25,000 feet, they entered the path of the jet stream, where screaming winds tried to tear them off of the side of the mountain. In those extremes, every detail had life or death consequences. Lou lost a shield to his glasses and, as a result of the wind and 20-degree temperatures, suffered almost total, though temporary, blindness after freezing his eyes.

Gregg Wilson broke a rib from coughing, since at that altitude there's not enough air pressure to fill the lungs and resist the force of a simple cough or sneeze. George Dunn, who without a stove had no way to melt snow, almost died from dehydration.

Dave Mahre said the twenty mile ascent from 16,500 feet to 21,300 feet over three days almost broke his will. But in working through the hardships, Mahre reflected the feelings of everyone involved, saying, "As part of the team, I felt I had to keep up my end of the bargain."

Because the climbers' fitness inevitably deteriorates above 18,000 feet, the team was racing against time to make the summit and return before suffering further disabilities. From the high camp of 26,600 feet, small parties set out four times to get to the top, and four times they had to turn back. On October 19, the high camp was occupied by John Roskelley, perhaps the premier high altitude climber in the world; Phil Ershler, who had been unsuccessful on Everest in two previous expeditions; and Jim Wickwire, a climber whose accomplishments included almost every major summit in the world except Everest. I'm talking about a Who's Who talent pool.

119

With the winter storms soon to arrive and with supplies and their physical condition being rapidly depleted, they knew that there would only be one more attempt possible on the next day. While Roskelley was committed to making the summit without the use of supplemental oxygen, there remained only one bottle of oxygen for use by either Ershler or Wickwire. To ensure success, one would have to use it, the other one would have to stay at high camp.

According to Wickwire, there ensued several hours of intense discussion between Ershler and him. Without making a decision, they slept fitfully for a few hours. In the early morning hours, with only a few spare words, it was decided that Ershler would take the oxygen and Roskelley would try to climb without it. Wickwire would stay behind and prepare for their return.

The going was slow and torturous. Ascending through a crumbling section of rock known as the Gray Band demanded technical climbing skills where just putting one foot in front of another required an enormous act of the will. With only a thousand feet to go but freezing from the inside out, Roskelley knew death was near. He had to return, or die. Whittaker said later, "When I saw John, he broke down saying, 'I gave it everything I had.'" Whittaker just shook his head and said, "No one could ask for anything more. It was a magnificent effort."

Without Roskelley, Ershler was now as isolated as any man could be on this earth. If something went wrong, there would be no help. He was on autopilot, concentrating on not making any mistakes. If he dropped his glove, he'd lose his fingers to the cold. He'd then lose his ice axe which would cause him to slip and lose his life. On the other hand, if just one of us reached the peak, in this case Ershler, we all would share in the success. We held our breath and whispered quiet prayers for his safety.

120

Down at base camp, cinematographer Steve Marts was following Ershler's progress through his big 1000 millimeter lens. Suddenly, Marts shouted, "He's waving his arms. He made it!" When

*Phil Ershler on the 1984
Everest summit.*

news arrived of Phil Ershler's successful summit attempt made on October 20, 1984, I bet our China-Everest crew cheered louder and made more noise than the crowd on opening night at Woodstock.

I'm sometimes asked what lessons I learned by participating in that extraordinary climb. While there are many insights to be pondered, at the top of my list is this: anyone can reach their dream or overcome a particular mountain in their life if they are willing to leave their comfort zone, work together with others, do their part with excellence, know their limits, stay "on mission," and share in the rewards when appropriate. I had always known these values. This climb, however, seared them into my spirit and provided a strong foundation for all of my subsequent business ventures.

If a prairie-grown, sandal-wearing hippie can find the inner resources to face a mountain the size of Everest, then *anything* is possible.

121

CAN YOU SAY KANGCHENJUNGA?

There are a variety of ways to spell Kangchenjunga, including: Kangchen Dzö-nga, Khangchendzonga, Kanchenjanga, Kachendzonga, or Kangchanfanga. Take your pick. Regardless of your choice, Kangchenjunga is one massive, man-eating mountain with five summits (the Nepalese call these the "Five Treasure Houses of the Snows").

By 1989, the year when our team started to ascend the world's third highest mountain, there had been seventy-five people from seventeen countries who had previously summitted Kangchenjunga's 28,146 feet. Twenty-five died trying. Put another way, one-in-three who try, die. Talk about sobering odds.

What's more, with this climb, we were attempting to do what no American team had done before. The idea for the trip actually struck Lou Whittaker in the spring of 1983 after his first attempt of Mt. Everest. Lou asked Senator Ted Kennedy to pull a few strings by writing a letter to then Prime Minister Indira Gandhi to see if we could get a permit for this restricted area. She graciously extended an invitation to Lou who, in 1988, received a permit for the South route. Our team had fourteen members, most of whom would be senior RMI guides, and a budget of $180,000—modest by any standard.

About the same time that Lou was seeking permission to climb Kangchenjunga, a Russian team was doing the same thing. They, too, were granted a permit, but for the North side. We learned that the Russians were amassing a huge crew of forty climbers and 1,000 porters. Since the South side would be an easier route for an entourage of that size, the Russians asked if Lou would consider trading permits. In truth, we preferred the Northern route and happily made the trade.

We had our permit and our preferred route. So far, so good. However, as eighteenth-century Scottish poet, Robert Burns, is attributed as saying, "The best-laid plans of mice and men often go awry." Unbeknown to us, we would soon experience the depth of his adage.

1989 Kangchenjunga team. Photo by Nawang Gombu.

This was no fault of Lou Whittaker, mind you. Lou had assembled a fantastic team of seasoned climbers: George Dunn, Phil Ershler, Nawang Gombu, Jim Hamilton, Craig Van Hoy, Robert Link, Larry Nielson, Dr. Howard Putter (the team physician), John Roskelley, Eric Simonson, Ed Viesturs, Jim Wickwire, Greg Wilson, Lou, and me.

While Himalayan experience wasn't a prerequisite, many of Lou's hand-picked team members had tasted what the Himalayans can dish out. The obstacles thrown into our path would be beyond our control. So, with the permit in hand, we got busy. Thanks to the participation by fifty-five sponsors and the sales of our very popular "Dancing Crampons" t-shirts, we were completely funded before we left. We sold upwards of $25,000 just in shirts. In my view, that's the toughest part of the climb—getting totally funded. Sure, we each had a seemingly endless list of other important details to chase down. But without the proper funding, we weren't going anywhere.

As we got closer to our departure, we bought $7,000 worth of our favorite foods. The idea was to eat at base camp pretty much the same things that we liked to eat at home. We'd pack corn flakes, oatmeal, peanut butter, honey, coffee—whatever folks enjoyed for breakfast that also gave them energy for the ascent. The same deal went for the other meals of the day. These food stuffs would be packed into 125 wax-coated boxes (to prevent moisture damage in the mountains) and had to weigh no more than sixty pounds each for the porters to carry.

We shipped the 125 boxes of food and supplies—all 3,500 pounds of it—by boat rather than by air to save almost $30,000. These essentials were scheduled to travel from Seattle to Calcutta where they would be trucked into Nepal and then carried into base camp. At least that was the plan.

Meanwhile, most of the team flew to Katmandu, the capital city of Nepal, where we spent several days pulling together the last minute details and logistics, not the least of which was hiring the porters. Because we were going into a restricted area, we wanted to set a good example in how we treated the environment. We planned to take everything out that we brought in. And, rather than burn the local timber for cooking, we made arrangements to carry propane tanks. As much as it was in our power, this would be a very clean expedition.

But, like I mentioned earlier, there would be a number of events that were clearly out of our power. Take the political scene. Here's where Robert Burn's poetry became a dark reality. If you were to look at a map, you'd find that Nepal is a small, land-

Craig Van Hoy and Phil Ershler on Kangchenjunga. Photo by Ed Viesturs.

locked country sandwiched between China to the north and India to the south. While awaiting the arrival of our 125 boxes of food and equipment in Katmandu, India and Nepal got into a serious trade disagreement. India promptly put the brakes on virtually all truck traffic at the Nepal border—including the truck carrying our necessities.

At that point, we had some of our personal gear but no familiar food. For the better part of a week, we had to survive off the local diet of eggs, rice, potatoes, and other foods most of which lacked iodine. Virtually everyone on the team got diarrhea or became sick due to the diet and food handling practices of the local cooks.

A WING AND A PRAYER

127

I've flown more than three million miles in my life. If you were to ask me which flight was the most unsettling, that would be easy. Hands down it would be that short flight from Katmandu to the nearby cliff side village of Taplejung on March 21, 1989. I was seated in a pint-sized Grumman prop plane with five friends and a pilot. Lou, as the driving force behind this adventure, assured us that taking this puddle jumper would cut about seven or eight days off our walk to base camp. I think it may have also shaved a few years off my life.

Sensing our apprehension, the pilot assured us his plane had STOL capabilities—also known as "short takeoff and landing." Grumman's are supposed to be adept at operating in tight quarters which was a real necessity on this trip. Taplejung's "airport" (elevation 3,000 feet) is not much more than a short, narrow grass airstrip perched along the edge of a cliff in the foothills of Kangchenjunga.

Our route of flight would take us within seventy miles of Everest, while cutting a careful path through the snow covered Himalayan mountain range to our destination. If all went as planned—and that was a big *if*—we would land on that unpaved, makeshift runway with a gapping drop off on one end. A slight miscalculation and our single-engine bird would be history. Thankfully, after a few heart-stopping banks and turns, we landed safely. However, the rusty remains of another airplane adjacent to the airport served to underscore the fact that even at this elevation, the mountain played for keeps.

For the better part of a week, we walked through the spectacular valleys and rivers that graced the lower altitudes of Kangchenjunga. Tall oaks, beautiful rhododendrons, dramatic sycamores, and grand magnolias created a canopy of deep greens and purples that were a feast for the eyes. We never tired of savoring each new stretch of forestry.

Rather than linger in the last village for our gear, Lou felt we should get started up the mountain to base camp which was several days away. We'd just pray that team member Eric Simonson, who had been traveling with the boxes once they arrived by boat in Calcutta, would find his way and meet us at base camp. With that decided, we loaded up into two Grumman planes and held on for the ride of our lives.

With the base camp positioned at 17,000 feet above sea level, the walk was the perfect way to acclimatize to the higher altitudes. As it turned out, Lou had us stop in Gunza, a village with just thirty people situated at 11,000 feet and located three days short of base camp. Lou learned that they had a Morse-code tele-graph key. For several days, Lou worked alongside of a Nepalese military guide (with Gombu translating Lou's comments) to reach Eric Simonson for a status report on our gear. But the information they got was more rumor than fact.

It was times like that when I was forced to learn real patience. Think about it. We were stuck in a foreign land largely cut off from the world. We had to wait around in a remote village with-out our food, equipment, or any motorized vehicles. Without any phones, our only connection to civilization was an antiquated tele-type machine. Not to mention that the nearest hospital was a sev-enteen-day trek if any of us were to become sick. Furthermore, we knew we didn't have an indefinite amount of time to just hang out with the monsoon rain season around the corner.

There's incredible pressure to do something, anything. That's when your patience is tested to the limits. Frankly, I'm grateful for that experience because it served me well in the years to come. I learned to be patient in my business dealings. Far too often, business-types want instant everything . . . and they want it *now*. I've discovered good things come to those who know how to be patient and wait.

For his part, team member Eric Simonson was having his patience tested, too. His truck with our 125 boxes was stuck in traffic behind 800 other trucks which had been refused permis-sion to cross from Calcutta into Nepal. Keep in mind that Eric is a seasoned professional. He's a world class adventurer who had conducted many of his own expeditions in the past. So, this wasn't his first rodeo, as the saying goes.

And yet, with our window of opportunity starting to close, Eric

129

needed a solution. He met a military official in the bathroom late at night where he did a little strategic palm-greasing. Five hundred dollars later, his supplies were approved to cross the border. The next day, Eric's vehicle moved from the back of the line of trucks to number three.

Once inside of Nepal, his next challenge was to locate a helicopter that would shuttle our gear to base camp. A couple of days went by without any luck. Disheartened yet determined, Eric finally found an operator who—for the tidy sum of $11,000—agreed to take three runs in with 75 of the 125 boxes. Something was better than nothing, right? Fortunately, Eric had a list of the contents of each box and knew he had to go with only the essentials. He cut the whiskey, the popcorn, and a lot of the food. At least we had our gear and climbing equipment.

In a remarkable display of self-sacrifice, Eric gave up his seat on the final helicopter trip so as to jam as much gear into the chopper as was possible. That act of good will on his part required Eric to forfeit his place on the climb. Ever the team player, his loss was our gain.

Once the base camp, our home for the next two months, was finally estab-

Kangchenjunga avalanche.
Photo by Skip Yowell.

130

lished, we joined the Nepalese for their traditional pre-climb prayer ceremony. They carefully strung up a number of prayer flags and read out of a book while burning Juniper wood to appease the gods. Of special concern were the number and frequency of the avalanches on Kangchenjunga which were the primary source of the high death ratio.

Speaking of avalanches, we saw and heard them peeling off every day; often they sounded like a runaway freight train barreling through the clefts. We were also asked to honor their request not to stand directly on the true summit for fear that we might offend their gods. We agreed and then set off on our climb. Our plan was to ascend on a fairly steep route to avoid the avalanches, while establishing a series of five camps for the final assault.

Once again, we hit another obstacle.

131

FROM RUSSIA WITH LOVE

It was now mid-April. We had weathered diarrhea and delays. Eric was out, and our food supply was thin. While setting up Camp II, Lou discovered a problem with the ten oxygen cylinders purchased in Katmandu—they had the wrong valve, which rendered them useless. While most of the guys didn't plan to use oxygen, Lou knew it was vital to have a minimal supply in case somebody got into trouble. Without supplemental oxygen, the prospects of reaching the summit dwindled.

Luckily, that's when a new thought hit us. The Russian team was making its ascent on the South side. Given the enormous size of their troop, they might be in a position to sell us some of their high tech bottles. Lou and Jim drafted a letter summarizing our need and then sent it to Ed Myslovsky, the Russian team leader. Of course, there was no easy way to do this—no FedEx, no mail, no transportation aside from walking.

We decided to send the request via Sherpa (a yak herdsman, often used as travel guides) along with $3,000 for the purchase. Assuming that the Sherpa was an honest man ($3,000 was more money than he could have made in a decade in that part of the world), the round trip trek from our base camp to the Russian camp would be sixteen days. But what choice did we have? Our patience was tested while we waited.

A hardy cheer erupted in the camp when the Sherpa returned carrying six bottles, two face masks, and a letter. In his letter, the Russian team leader returned our money, saying, "We think that the air is not to sell. It doesn't depend on whether it is the air from Moscow or Seattle, so we are happy to send you some air from Russia. Have a safe climb." He also mentioned that they wanted the empties upon our return—and asked us to buy them "much whiskey" back in Katmandu upon our mutually safe return, which we gladly did.

We were back in business. But that wasn't the end of our string of setbacks. Upon reaching Camp IV, both Jim Wickwire (the first American to climb K2) and John Roskelley contracted pneumonia and had to descend to base camp. That was a real blow, especially since John had prior experience on Kangchenjunga. Making matters worse, Jim Hamilton hurt his shoulder so he was knocked off the climb.

At this juncture, we had lost four of the fourteen team members we started with and our medical supplies were running dry. In fact, Dr. Howard Putter, our team physician, actually ran out of medicine due to the level of illness throughout the expedition. He had to rely on the drugs brought along by Ed Viesturs who was a veterinarian by trade. You might say that our health care went to the dogs.

Not long afterwards, we ran out of food. All we had to sustain us were candy bars—hardly the Breakfast of Champions. I ultimately lost thirty pounds on this climb. It took a full nine months for me to regain my weight and strength. In spite of the delays, the string of obstacles, the hassles, and the loss of almost a third of our team, we didn't give up. We encouraged each other and dug in for the final push before the nasty monsoon storms arrived with their unforgiving blasts of snow.

I CAN SEE FOR MILES AND MILES

On May 18, 1989, Phil Ershler, Craig Van Hoy, and Ed Viesturs were up at high camp. Just before the crack of dawn they radioed down to report that it was a pristine day and a comfortable twenty degrees. They decided to take off for the summit at 6 a.m. By 1 p.m., they reached the summit. As they would later report, the splendor of the surrounding mountain peaks draped in snow was simply majestic. They were the first Americans to join the ranks of the few who set foot atop that amazing wonder of God's creation.

Interestingly, they found a couple of oxygen bottles indicating that the Russians had made it, too. Several days later, on May 21, 1989, Robert Link, Larry Nielson, and Greg Wilson (all Rainier mountaineer guides) braved the blowing snow and heavy cloud cover to reach the Kangchenjunga summit, an unbelievable feat considering the opposition we faced almost every step of the way.

While there are many lessons to take away from the American Kangchenjunga Expedition Team, the primary one for me was this: *never underestimate the value of teamwork.* When a group of compatible, professional individuals combine their resources and skills, and when they are willing to be self-sacrificing as needed, no challenge is too great and no obstacle is too difficult.

I believe that dynamic is what we experience at JanSport. Like a well-oiled machine, a strong team learns to ebb, to flow, and to adapt to the challenges that will invariably come. They're receptive to new ideas. They know how to listen to and respect one another. They set aside their personal agenda for the greater good, as Eric did when he forfeited his spot on the climb.

Ed Viesturs and Phil Ershler on a Kangchenjunga summit at 28,169 feet. Photo by Craig Van Hoy.

In similar fashion, while it may be tempting to ascend the corporate ladder solo, the chances of your success increase exponentially if you attract teammates along the way. On that score, I'd have to disagree with Simon and Garfunkel when they sang, "I am a rock, I am an island."

But, before moving on to the next chapter, there's one additional part of the story I must share. While the monsoon graciously waited for us to make history, it did its darndest to make us miserable on the way off the mountain. Remember that serene 120 mile hike in through the lush forest canopy? Forget about it. The heavy monsoon rains brought a host of bloodsucking leeches that dropped on us with heat seeking accuracy. Even at night there was no escape.

You see, leeches are genetically hard-wired to sense the presence of warm-blooded creatures—that included us. I'll never forget the first evening when a virtual army of those slimy parasites crawled into our tent. By the morning, they were affixed to our necks, earlobes, arms—you name it. Each time someone would attempt to brush one off, the engorged leech would burst and smear its feast of blood everywhere.

You know what? That's another reason why a team effort is more desirable than going solo . . . try picking leeches off your back by yourself!

135

13

YOU'VE GOT A FRIEND

Spouting hip slogans about love, peace, and alternative mental states was a big a part of the Sixties movement. Whether bare-footed in Berkeley or burning bras in Boston, hippies everywhere were fond of saying, "Give peace a chance," "Make love, not war," "Tune in, turn on, drop out," and, "Don't trust anybody over thirty." Evidently, we didn't have the foresight to anticipate what would happen once *we* hit thirty. Still, when taken together, these popular slogans formed the collective tapestry of thought embraced by the New Generation.

Just as the Sixties had a set of phrases defining the hippie philosophy, climbing the corporate ladder comes with its own peculiar set of buzz words and advice as espoused by today's moti-vational gurus. Just thumb through the current crop of popular books on reaching the top rung. To successfully ascend the ladder, you and I are told we must:

Find ways to toot your own horn

Learn how to butter up coworkers

Schmooze or lose

Use or be used

Fight to stay in the loop

Master office politics

Strive to be recognized as better than those around you

While I won't go out of my way to criticize folks who operate within such a self-limiting mindset, climbing the corporate ladder under those guidelines sure sounds like a downer.

I've taken a different path. In my view, to become successful in business is not a product of "looking out for Number One." On the contrary, I believe it's important that *while you pursue your own dreams, it is equally important to support the dreams of others*.

Put another way, what's missing from the vernacular of today's business climbing advice books are three simple ideas. And believe it or not, these three ideas or values actually have their roots in the hippie culture. I'm talking about *nurturing others*, *speaking well of others*, and *assisting others*. A person who exhibits that kind of generous spirit in the workplace is bound to stand out.

Let's take the matter of *nurturing others*. When an employee in good standing at JanSport decides to leave our team, I've made it my practice to help them as best I can to land on their feet. Why? I enjoy being the kind of person who invests in and nurtures others. To that end, I've actually called our competitors to pave the way if we've got a good person who plans to leave JanSport. What's the value in that? It's simple: Good comes around.

Obviously, I don't want someone to work at JanSport if they're unhappy or unfulfilled. Both they and JanSport will not win in a relationship like that. However, if I can assist them as they seek to find the right job fit elsewhere, then I still have a friend long after they're off of our payroll. I don't know about you, but in this life I can use all the friends I can make—and keep.

This relates to the second part of the hippie approach to business: *speaking well of others.* I doubt you will ever hear me say something bad about a competitor. Maybe that's part of the hippie worldview of "live and let live." Maybe it's bad Karma to bad mouth others. Whatever the psychology, that's how I'm wired. Granted, I might point out how JanSport is different from our competition or how JanSport provides a better warranty or product solution.

But there's never a need for me to speak poorly of another person or company. Speaking in an unkind fashion about another individual is both unprofessional and reflects poorly on the person speaking. Besides, taking the high road always gives a better view. In a nutshell, I try to say something helpful or I'll say nothing at all.

The third part of my approach to climbing the corporate ladder is *assisting others* by helping them reach their goals and dreams. Let's look at that for a moment.

MOUNTAINS AND T-SHIRTS

I first met Ed Viesturs on a JanSport dealer climb up Mt. Rainier. Ed was one of the RMI guides that we worked with to lead our guests to the summit. From the start I could tell that Ed was just a wonderful, quality person. He would do anything he could to make our dealers feel welcomed, comfortable, and capable of the climb. Ed was truly the kind of guy who would give you the shirt off his back.

Then in 1989, Ed was one of my teammates on a climb up Mt. Kangchenjunga, also known as the Five Treasures of the Snow. Straddling Nepal and India's Himalayan range with its jagged, icy profile, Kangchenjunga actually has five breathtaking peaks, four of which are higher than 8,000 meters. Not only is Kangchenjunga the world's third highest mountain, it sports some of the most spectacular 6,000 and 7,000 meter peaks.

When Ed climbed Kangchenjunga in '89, it was his first 8,000 meter peak without the aid of supplemental oxygen. The following year, Ed went on to climb Mt. Everest without supplemental oxygen. Having scaled the world's first and third highest mountains without oxygen, Ed thought it would be a cool idea to scale K2, the world's second highest mountain as well.

So in 1992, Ed teamed up with a renowned climber out of Seattle, Scott Fischer, to summit K2. But Ed was out of a job and he needed to raise the funds for his expedition. It was then that Ed remembered how we had raised funds for the initial Kangchenjunga expedition by selling t-shirts. Ed called me and shared his dream of scaling K2. He then asked if we would come up with the logo and shirt design, print them up, and ship them out to him. He said he'd obviously pay us back—at our cost. And believe it or not, I agreed.

But why would anybody agree to a deal like that? Sure, Ed's dream was cool—only a handful of mountaineers had climbed the top three mountains without oxygen. But it was still *his* dream. Besides, we'd be providing the shirts at our cost; in other words, there was no money in it for us. Again, why do it? It sure would have been less hassle for us to turn him down. I believe that while you pursue your own dreams, it is equally important to support the dreams of others.

Scott and Ed finally reached the point of their departure by scraping together enough money from t-shirt sales, by charging their credit cards, and by selling whatever else they could find of value. While on the plane flying to Kathmandu, Ed realized that he hadn't paid the $15,000 t-shirt bill to JanSport. That weighed heavily on him through his whole expedition, which was four months long. Being a man of his word, Ed hosted a number of slideshows upon his return featuring photos from his climb and quickly raised the $15,000 to pay us back.

AMERICAN
SOVIET
K
2
92
EXPEDITION

October 14, 1992

Dear Skip,
    Scott and I would like to thank you again for supporting our K-2 Expedition. It was people like you that made it all possible. We have enclosed an expedition report and a signed photo of K-2. The route that we climbed was the right hand skyline.

Very Truly Yours,

Ed Viesturs

Scott Fischer

In this case, my investment in Ed's dreams would later serve as the basis of his desire to become a JanSport athlete, helping us design and endorse our technical products, which was no small matter. In the years that followed his successful K2 ascent, Ed became the first American to summit each of the fourteen 8,000 meter mountains in the world without oxygen. He was the 12th person in history to accomplish that incredible feat. Because we helped him, he continues to help us to this day.

LIVE TO TELL

Speaking of investing in others, here is another example. Meet Amber Brookman. Amber is an attractive blonde who started out as a model in Los Angeles. She continued her career in modeling with a relocation to New York City. With an eye on using both her brains and her good looks, she took a job at Allied Fabrics in public relations and product development work. I met Amber at a tradeshow in 1981 where I discussed our specific fabric needs for our daypacks at JanSport.

Several weeks later, Amber called and told me she was going to visit a number of her customers that were using Allied's products. She offered to stop by our factory and the operation in Everett because she thought there might be a way Allied could meet our specialized fabric needs. Grateful for the interest from this big time New York firm, we scheduled a visit. The fact that she was a former model had absolutely *nothing* to do with our getting together. Okay, well maybe a little.

Just for the fun of it, I decided to rent a limo when the day arrived. I told Murray, "You're coming with me. Today we're going to pick up Amber Brookman in style." I had never done this before. This was an all-time first. We arrived at the Westin Hotel in downtown Seattle, picked up Amber, drove around, shared some laughs—and a few beers. After lunch, we toured parts of Puget Sound. We never did make it to the factory. We were just too busy enjoying her company.

That afternoon as we dropped Amber off, I told her I would pick her up for dinner that night. At the time, I owned an old, beat-up 1934 International pickup. I decided it would be a real hoot to drive that beater truck downtown to take Amber to a very nice restaurant on Capitol Hill. When I pulled up to the Westin Hotel in my trusty but rusty pickup, Amber was waiting on the sidewalk, dressed very nicely. I'm not quite sure what she was thinking since we went from the limo to the 1934 pickup.

During dinner, I told Amber about our dealer climb on Mt. Rainier and said that she really ought to join us because that would get her involved with the outdoor industry and related businesses. She stirred her drink while casting me a skeptical eye. "Are we going to have camp-fires? Will we be roasting marsh-mallows?" she asked with a playful smirk.

"No," I said, but quickly added, "You'll have a great time, that I can promise." I had learned that she was into skiing but that she had never done any mountain climbing.

Amber Brookman and Skip during a 1980s Mt. Rainier seminar.

143

Being the good sport that she was, Amber agreed to consider my offer.

As the time for the climb approached, I mailed Amber and the other climbers the equipment list. She responded back and asked, "Now, Skip, what is the ice ax for? Is that for stirring a martini?"

I was pleasantly surprised that Amber agreed to come. That first year, although she was a real trouper and did her best, she didn't make it to the summit. Being the competitive, driven person that she is, Amber signed up to return and try again. One of the things we still joke about today was her interpretive approach to our training.

For example, we teach something known as the "rest step." This is where you take a step and you pressure breathe to keep the oxygen going through your lungs instead of the hurried up pace that is an extension of our busy lives. The rest step offers a very nice, relaxed pace. Amber, though, would do the "model step" which was kind of a unique shuffle more suitable for a fashion show runway. We'd say, "Amber you're doing the 'model step' and you need to do the 'rest step.'" I'm not sure if she ever did make the transition.

The second year, Amber returned and was on Lou Whittaker's rope at the back of his four-person team. My rope team followed Lou's group which meant that I was traveling behind Amber. Our typical early morning start required us to have our headlamps on. We left Camp Muir at 10,000 feet, traveled up and over Cathedral Rocks, headed to Cleaver and watched the sun as it started to rise in the east. While a beautiful sight to watch from an elevation of 13,000 feet, it can create a visually difficult scenario. Without warning, Amber fell through a crevasse.

Now, I have fallen into a crevasse and I can promise you that you don't want to. They are tricky to spot. You might be walking along and suddenly fall into a big hole that had been covered up. Many times they're open, in which case you can see and avoid them. But, there are times when they're concealed.

Part of our training is that if somebody falls down a crevasse, everyone else on the rope team must go down into a self-arrest with their ice ax, and stop the fall. That's step one. Step two is to pull that individual out of the crevasse.

From my vantage point, I watched as Amber dropped down and begun to sway back and forth like a rag doll puppet. I think it's safe to say her screams echoed off of Mt. Saint Helens forty miles away. I wouldn't be surprised if she wet her pants. It's scary stuff. Of course, Lou and his team went into self-arrest. Lou's big, booming voice called out, "Don't worry, Amber, we're going to pull you out."

Although she accidentally released and lost her ice ax down into the crevasse, we managed to pull her to safety. With the summit just one more hour away, Amber didn't want to turn back. We pressed on. Given how spiked her adrenaline was, Amber talked non-stop all the way to the top.

Something magical happened to Amber that day. Just as we had experienced on previous climbs, she, too, had been changed by the mountain. Amber stared death in the face, dug deep within her soul to find a strength that had been kept tucked away, and then finished what she started. From that day forward, no mountain, no obstacle, no challenge, whether real or imagined, would ever appear insurmountable again.

I'd like to think that Amber's mountaintop experience with us

145

somehow gave her the inner courage to leave Allied Fabrics, as she did, to pursue her own set of dreams. Amber went on to become the founder, CEO, and president of Brookwood Companies, a textile and apparel company with annual sales of more than one hundred thirty million dollars. We still partner with her company to this day.

As you might imagine, Amber continues to spread the good word about her transforming experience with JanSport. As you invest in others, they invest in you. Thankfully, there was a time early on in JanSport history when one of our competitors practiced this nurturing philosophy toward us.

146

Ed Viesturs took this picture of himself on the Himalayan summit.

RUNNING ON EMPTY

If you were to trace the history of the rigid frame pack back to its roots, you'd bump into the broad shoulders of Lloyd F. Nelson.

In the Spring of 1920, Lloyd was working at the Puget Sound Navel Shipyard in the Pacific Northwest. During a brief leave from work, he decided to cross an Alaskan mountain range on foot. Back then, hikers only had a basic canvas sack with shoulder straps to lug gear.

As Lloyd prepared for the trek, an Indian friend lent him a traditional Indian pack board. This somewhat crude design featured sealskin stretched around several willow sticks. While an improvement over the limp canvas sack, his back ached for weeks. Over the next nine years, Lloyd worked nights in his basement to perfect a rigid frame pack using wood slats and canvas. He ultimately developed a pack known as the "Trapper Nelson" that did a good job of distributing the weight. It was certainly a real improvement over anything on the market.

He got the patent for his rigid frame pack design, and in 1929 sold the business to Charles Trager, a Seattle-based manufacturer of equipment for the lumberjack and mining industries. It wouldn't be long before Trager's company experienced remarkable sales of the "Trapper Nelson" pack, the industry standard for several decades. From the Boy Scouts of America and the U.S. Forest Service to the U.S. Army Mapping Service, Trager supplied Trapper Nelson pack boards to an ever-growing market that would ultimately include REI and Eddie Bauer.

Charles Trager passed the business on to his son George. While I never met Charles, George and I developed a friendship over the years. You see, during the very early days of JanSport, we would often run out of raw material to make our flexible frame pack. Since Trager's outfit was across town, we introduced ourselves to George Trager. George took a liking to us young guys

147

with long hair—so much so that when we ran out of materials he'd say, "Skip, just borrow what you need and be sure and pay me back as soon as you can."

For the next several years, Murray and I borrowed bolts of fabric and grommets as needed and repaid George as quickly as we could from our profits. Keep in mind we were technically competitors. Why should George have helped a couple of hippies? What was in it for him? In his own way, George played an important part in the JanSport story. His kindness was one of the stepping stones which enabled JanSport to become the global leader that it is today.

His unconventional generosity which led to the success of our fledging company is an example of what happens when a business man or woman decides to *nurture others*, *speak well of others*, and *assist others*. I carry with me a fond memory of how George believed in us and helped us out when we needed it most. Not surprisingly, that is exactly the kind of business leader I strive to be.

Maybe George was a hippie at heart after all.

BARE-CHESTED IN BHUTAN

I've made a habit of stretching myself. I frequently push myself to engage in experiences that are way outside my comfort zone. No, I'm *not* a glutton for punishment. However, I've found expanding my horizons and taking advantage of unusual opportunities keeps me sharp when I'm back once again at my desk in the office. I find I'm energized by rich, new experiences I've had and by the memories I've made. The sights, sounds, smells, and people I've met on my adventure refill my creative tank to overflowing.

I don't want to make the mistake of reaching the "top floor" with the corner office, the plush carpet, and a sweeping view of the city lights and think that I have really arrived. I think what's needed is to keep in touch with the soil that clings to my roots. In time, isolated executives will stagnate. Getting a little dirt under manicured fingernails does a person a lot of good.

So, when I sense I'm becoming dull, lifeless, unmotivated, or redundant in the workplace, I take that as a sign that I've got to

149

get out. That explains why I have traveled to some remarkable places in my life. I'm not talking about remarkable as in touristy, "been there, done that, got the T-shirt" destinations. I mean those rare, life-changing, remote spots which are so striking, I feel as if I am standing next to Moses on sacred ground.

This also explains why I was intrigued by a phone call from my good friend Nawang Gombu, the Sherpa. Gombu is the nephew of Tenzing Norgay who accompanied Sir Edmund Hillary on his first summit of Mt. Everest in 1953.

Gombu knows a thing or two about high adventure, too. As a youngster, Gombu's parents sent him away to live at Rombuk Monastery. Located just below Mt. Everest's base camp on the Tibetan side, his new home was situated at a breath-denying 11,000 feet, making Rombuk one of the highest monasteries in the world. Since Gombu was to become a monk, his cheeks were routinely beaten as part of his discipline, at times causing his mouth to swell up so much he was unable to eat.

One night, Gombu and a friend decided they had had enough and didn't want any more of this regiment. Together they planned their escape. Keep in mind, Gombu was surrounded by deep snow, he had no formal mountain climbing training, and he didn't have a cool stash of outdoor gear suitable for the trip. Never one to give up on a challenge, Gombu suggested that they tie rope around their sandals—yes, sandals—for added traction in the snow. After five days of traversing a 20,000 foot mountain pass, Gombu arrived safely home.

Not bad for an eleven-year-old.

Clearly, Gombu was destined to be a professional climber. In 1953, he served as a Sherpa on the first Everest expedition with

Sir Edmund Hillary and Tenzing, carrying a backbreaking load of gear to a height of 27,000 feet. Years later, in 1963, Gombu worked with Jim Whittaker, the first American to summit Everest. Gombu became the first person to climb Everest twice, the second time came in 1965 on an Indian Expedition. His accomplishments were so grand, he was awarded the Hubbard medal of honor by President John F. Kennedy.

As you can imagine, when a guy like Gombu has an idea for a great adventure, it's sure to be something special. In 1995, Gombu called to invite my wife Winnie and me, as well as Lou and Ingrid Whittaker, to join him on the trip of a lifetime: a visit to the mysterious and magical country of Bhutan. The opportunity appealed to me for two reasons. First of all, as you know, I'm an adventurer at heart. Gombu knows of my love for the outdoors and knows how these excursions stimulate in me new business ideas.

Secondly, Bhutan is a modern enigma. Up until 1960, Bhutan's borders were closed to outsiders, its self-imposed isolation the by-product of a monarch who quite understandably didn't want his slice of utopia to become another cookie cutter kingdom. He also recognized his land-locked nation didn't have the infrastructure to deal with an increase in tourism.

A mere three thousand guests are granted admission each year to enter this Garden of Eden-like country. The select few who are permitted entrance must travel with government-sanctioned tour operators. So, while getting into Bhutan is not as rare as owning a copy of the 1963 Beatles album, *Please, Please Me*, signed by Ringo, John, George, and Paul—of which there are less than half a dozen verified copies in the United States—possessing a coveted invitation to visit Bhutan certainly comes close.

151

Part of the appeal of this tiny kingdom in southern Asia is the way they have managed to repel virtually all twenty-first-century influences. There are no Starbucks. No fast food joints selling Yakburgers. No FedEx. No vending machines. No malls. Not even email. In Bhutan, western clothing takes a back seat to wearing the native dress. Only a few watch television. After all, the first TV sets were not introduced until 1999. Considering that the average annual income is just $1,300 U.S. dollars, few Bhutanese are in a hurry to mount a big screen on their hut wall. Especially since many don't even have a bed. Besides, there's just one TV station in the country.

You might be tempted to think that their effort to prevent the encroachment of outside influences is narrow-minded. Maybe. But I believe there's something refreshing about living in a country where people don't have the foggiest idea what Madonna's belly-

button looks like.

With less than a handful of paved roads, the Bhutanese have yet to string their first stop light. Their one and only airport *does* have a paved runway, but commercial pilots must receive specialized flight training to navigate the heart-pounding, final approach over the jaw-like Himalayan foothills. Indeed, Bhutan is one of

Children carrying their goods through the village. Photo by Skip Yowell.

the world's last pristine gems, a true one-of-a-kind destination. The people of Bhutan are lost in time, and they like it that way.

LAND OF THE DRAGON

Gombu's home is tucked away in the mountains of Darjeeling, India. The Kingdom of Bhutan just happens to sit to the north of his mountain retreat, which doubles as a training ground for climbers. As the Director of the Himalayan Mountaineering Institute, Gombu had connections with Jigme Singye Wangchuck the king of Bhutan. Through that unique relationship, Gombu arranged for us to visit Druk Yul—which means "The Land of the Dragon"—as the locals call Bhutan.

Winnie and I packed our bags and hiking gear and headed halfway around the globe. Getting from the United States to Bhutan offered its own set of adventures. We had to fly to Bangkok, to Calcutta, and then on to Bhutan. We used part of our extended travel time to research the topography and history of this special country which hadn't changed much in hundreds of years.

We learned Bhutan has three major and diverse land regions sandwiched into an area that's half the size of the state of Indiana. The south is characterized by rolling plains and deep, lush river valleys. Just north of the valleys, the Himalayan foothills rise sharply like a giant staircase from 5,000 to 14,000 feet—you might say it resembles the original Stairway to Heaven. This ultimately gives way to snow and glacier-covered, rugged mountainous highlands that top out at 24,000 feet above sea level. Taken together, these regions produce an amazing variety of climate conditions.

We learned that while there are no neighborhood Home Depots, the Bhutanese still manage to build their own houses. But you can forget about air conditioning or electricity in most of them. We're talking candles for light with heat in the winter produced by burning dried yak dung in a wood burning stove. Even their farm animals are allowed to live inside their homes as if they were part of the family.

We also learned that the Bhutanese raise their own crops and, when the crops come in during harvest time, they throw a giant party complete with festival dances every year. The young and old wear beautiful, hand-crafted wooden masks and play a variety of wooden instruments to celebrate the bounty. This I had to see. I mean, having grown up in the heart of Kansas' grain fields, I can say with some authority I've never seen American farmers engage in an annual harvest shindig. About as close as they might come to the Bhutan's festivity is to pop open a few Buds after parking their John Deere combines for the winter.

Then I read aloud to Winnie the fact that the king has four wives who all happen to be sisters. As I mull this over, Winnie gave me the evil eye which, in any language, could be translated: "You aren't a Bhutanese king and you can just forget about that idea, buster." I offered a sheepish grin as if to suggest, *The thought never crossed my mind, dear.*

Turning back to my reading material, I noted that marijuana grows freely in the countryside, but there's no drug traffic or resident pot heads—probably because there are no Beatle albums. Instead, the farmers feed the marijuana to their pigs because it increases their appetite. This made sense. It explained why the pot smoking hippies back in the Sixties used to get the munchies.

I made a mental note to add that to my "Fun Facts From Skip's Almanac."

Our plan was to climb, travel, and experience as much of this remarkable culture as we could squeeze into the trip. Keep in mind that Bhutan is the last country that's all Buddhist. The centerpiece of our time, then, would be to hike up to the Tiger's Nest Buddhist monastery which clings to the side of the mountain like a gecko. Tiger's Nest, better known to the locals as Taktsang Dzong, is perched 9,000 feet above sea level, a feat of ancient construction that boggles the mind.

All of the building supplies had to be carried up on the backs of donkeys or yaks. There were no roads and the workers had no power tools or electricity. Nor was there space for scaffolding; the back of the monastery rests against a sheer rock wall on one side. The front of the two-story structure sits precisely on the edge of a

Tiger's Nest in Bhutan. Photo by Skip Yowell.

cliff that drops down thousands of feet to the river below. I had to wonder, *Why build a monastery there?*

According to legend, the Buddhist monk Guru Rimpoche brought Buddhism from Tibet to Bhutan by riding on the back of a flying, flaming tiger. He touched down on this unlikely cliff-side spot anointing it the building site of choice. I guess in this magical world, that might be believable. In any case, today's monks will live at Tiger's Nest for three years at a time. I assumed we would not be permitted to set foot anywhere near the monastery— it is typically forbidden—but because we were with Gombu, we would be allowed to enter. I knew that seeing this world famous house of worship and its unusual customs from the adjacent cliff would be unforgettable.

After our plane landed, I found that everything we had read about Bhutan didn't tell half of the story. Winnie and I were overwhelmed by the gracious people we met, many of whom spoke English, the colorful sights of their handmade articles, and the radically different environment in which we found ourselves. Standing there in the midst of that centuries-old culture felt . . . *other worldly*. We knew we were still on Earth, but that secluded stretch of enchanting land almost defied description. Gombu was right. This would be an unforgettable time of discovery.

Within minutes of our arrival, I could feel the untapped portions of my mind stirring from their slumber and being put to good use. The creative synapses started to fire on all cylinders as my brain, like a sponge, sopped up each new, unexpected sensation. This magical mystery tour was exactly what I needed and I eagerly embraced every moment as if it were an old friend.

THE GREAT AWAKENING

JanSport, like any business, is driven by creative ideas. Ideas lead to innovation. In that respect, ideas are the clay from which new products, better marketing strategies, and increased market share are fashioned. Ideas fuel growth. There is nothing like a unique idea to keep us ahead of the competition. Not only that, a good idea can prevent missteps. The daily challenge is to constantly generate a fresh source of winning ideas.

As I said at the outset, there are times when I find that I have very little raw, unprocessed material left stored inside of my "experience tank." In those moments, I find myself running on fumes. Frankly, as one who has been thrust into the corporate environment quite by accident, I'll be the first to admit that it's tempting to be comfortably stuck in the rut of prior accomplishments and rely upon well-worn ways of tackling issues. The corporate environment tends to have that effect.

The bigger a company gets, the greater the pressure to play things safe and do things *like everybody else*, especially if you are blessed by being one of the top leaders in your field. There the stakes are much higher and, like heavily milled flour, all of the new ideas have been bleached out before they can surface and do some real damage.

What's the end result? *Imitation* rather than *innovation*. Rather than allow ideas the free reign to take us into the deep, uncharted waters, we restrict them to the shallow end of the pool. That's where everybody is huddled together or perhaps playing Marco Polo. In business, this is the tendency to identify what's "hot" or "in" and then just imitate that idea instead of pushing the

157

limits and testing the waters. No wonder so many products lack originality, style, and class.

As I see it, here's the bottom line. You and I have two choices when it comes to doing business: *innovation or imitation*. Yes, to imitate what the competition is doing carries fewer risks. But I believe the innovator is the one who will reap the rewards if he takes the more difficult path. Let me illustrate with a story.

One hot, sticky afternoon I took a walk around the unpaved, dusty streets of Bhutan. I took my shirt off, as I often do when I'm outdoors. While a white man with hair on his chest is no big deal in America, being bare-chested in a place like Bhutan is another matter. Many there have never seen a man with body hair. Aside from what's on their heads, the Bhutanese are not a hairy people.

With a shy, tentative motion, people would stop and glance in my direction clearly intrigued by the patch of hair between my pecs. I had a similar reaction while visiting in nearby Tibet— only in that instance, the locals flocked around and ran their fingers across my chest trying to figure out why hair was growing there. Other visitors were not accosted in such a way because they kept their shirts on and they looked pretty much like everyone else. The moment something or someone really different arrived on the scene, the locals were stirred to curiosity and action.

What's the bottom line? You and I always have a choice. Our businesses can follow the safe, predictable routes others have taken, or they can distinguish themselves by standing bare-chested—the unusual next to the typical. To stand out in a crowd, we must commit ourselves to the quest of true innovation. That's what will make others sit up and take notice. That's the path we at JanSport have chosen.

My best advice, then, is to consider the Bhutanese. Look at the sharp cliffs of the Himalayans. Forget the obstacles. Don't be afraid of the risks. Then go build or invent something that the world will marvel at centuries later. Don't think it can be done? Tell that to the monks living in Tiger's Nest 9,000 feet above sea level on the side of a cliff.

159

EASY RIDER MEETS CAPTAIN AMERICA

*I*n 1964, when Dylan sang the times were "a-changin'," that was both an understatement and a foreshadowing of things to come. From politics to art, nonconformist hippies sought to change the world. Take fashion, for example. Hippies rejected most of the commercially produced options of the day. If skirts were long, hippies grabbed scissors and shortened them into mini-skirts—which scandalized traditional sensibilities everywhere. Then, almost as an afterthought, they lengthened them into sandal-hugging maxi-skirts.

When it came to white t-shirts, the vanilla-look was good enough for the kids with crew cuts in Sears catalogues, but hippies—known for their flamboyant tastes—crinkled those bland white shirts by the fistful, dipped them in exotic colors, and introduced the tie-dyed look. If pant legs were straight, they flared the cuff and—voilà!—bell bottoms were born. And, just for kicks, a bolt of fabric was added to the lower third of the pant leg, expanding the bell bottoms into "elephant bells." What's more, waist-high jeans were out; low riding hip-huggers were in.

Fringes, patches, buttons, and beads—each added a splash of color, made a statement or, in some other way, reflected the personality of the individual. After all, self-expression was king, man. I developed a sense of personal style early on. You might say I always wanted to "look sharp," using *my* ideas of what that meant.

When I was in 7th grade, I remember riding in the family sedan as my mom took me out for a little back to school shopping. On the drive over to the store, I had a hunch we might not see eye-to-eye on her selections. And sure enough, all of mom's choices would have marked me for life as hopelessly "fashion-challenged."

After dutifully trying on her clothing picks, I told my mother how much I appreciated her ideas but said I couldn't wear "those clothes." Mom was cool. She wisely told me to go buy my own clothes. Thankfully, I have always been a saver and had saved money from shoveling snow, paper routes, and odd jobs.

From that day on, I bought all my own clothing. Mom's decision to let me express myself helped me to appreciate the different styles offered, to study the quality of the goods, and to keep an eye on the price. (Back then, a good pair of Lee jeans was $4.25—which was a lot of money.)

It's no wonder, then, that years later, JanSport added fashion to the functionality of our products. Being fashionable was a natural extension of how I was wired. It was also a reflection of the times that we lived in. To remain competitive, we knew we had to be innovative. And to be innovative, we had to keep our ear to the ground and listen carefully to the direction of the fashion trends of the day. That's still the case today.

Here's an example. When it came to frame packs in the Sixties, everything in the market was pretty conservative—dark green or drab brown canvas ruled. Since we hippies were a little on the irreverent side and knew the hippie mindset, we pushed the line in the fashion department. One of our first packs, for instance, sported a psychedelic collection of colorful daisies. It just seemed so fun to take the traditional pack and deck it out in flowers. Talk about a huge hit with the hippie crowd.

1970 JanSport frame pack. Photo by Skip Yowell.

That design was so popular back then that we recently reintroduced it to a whole new generation that happens to be into the retro look. It's been a best-seller. Another hands-down favorite pack design drew its fashion inspiration from an encounter with a cultural icon, Peter Fonda. Once again, by paying close attention to the cultural trends, we hit a homerun with our Captain America pack.

163

FASHION, FILM, AND THE FUTURE

When Dennis Hopper and Peter Fonda rode their hopped-up Harleys in the 1969 hit movie, *Easy Rider*, they cemented their place in hippie history. Playing the part of two long-haired renegades who "went looking for America but couldn't find it anywhere," Hopper and Fonda became poster boys of the counterculture. Sampling freely of the drugs, the women, and the good times, they cruised from California to New Orleans in hopes of making it in time for Mardi Gras. Now, I would like to mention that while the movie captured the freewheeling spirit of the Sixties, the drugs used were not the path I'd chosen. I preferred the natural high from hanging out in the great outdoors.

With Steppenwolf's hard-driving "Born to Be Wild" anthem fueling the soundtrack, Fonda's character, Wyatt, burst on the scene wearing a patriotic red, white, and blue helmet. Sporting similar markings on his California-style chopper and wearing an American flag-festooned leather jacket, Wyatt twice introduced himself as "Captain America" in the film. His rugged individualism and freedom-loving spirit was immediately cherished by hippies everywhere. The movie was such a big hit that the colors red, white, and blue became very popular—a trend we immediately picked up on.

On the heels of *Easy Rider*, Peter Fonda directed a low budget sci-fi film of his own called, *Idaho Transfer*. The film's scriptwriter, Thomas Matthiesen, was a college acquaintance of Murray's who commissioned JanSport to make an assortment of *unusual*—code word for weird—red, white, and blue framepacks and daypacks for use in the movie. We were told that the script had an "end of the world" feel to it. Our job was to design something futuristic that would work with their theme.

Filmed in a warehouse in Bellevue, Washington and on location in Craters of the Moon, Idaho, Murray and I had the chance to be on the set during the shoot and to visit with Peter Fonda. After meeting Peter, we had the inspiration that we needed. What emerged was our "Captain America" pack that was ultimately featured in the film. Originally, we silk screened stars and stripes onto the pocket fabric of the pack. The demand for our Captain America pack became so strong, we switched to pack cloth with the patriotic design already printed. The pack was

165

Murray and Skip with the Captain America pack on Mt. Rainier. Photo by Marsha Burns.

very successful with more than 25,000 sold during its two-year lifespan.

Since then, JanSport has grown a lot. We've expanded our product line from fashionable framepacks to book bags and day-packs to travel packs. We've sponsored major expedition climbs from Everest to Kangchenjunga. And we've met some pretty incredible people and a few nasty bears along the way. The principles we held fast to in the beginning—adding fun, fashion, and function to high quality gear—are what JanSport stands for today.

We still make the best quality outdoor gear possible. We still believe in getting outdoors whenever we can. In the mountains, in nature, or just out hiking around, we learn a lot about quality, durability, and the features that consumers are asking for. And we still keep our ear to the pavement to identify new trends.

WIRED FOR SOUND

Back in 2002, JanSport introduced the "LiveWire" pack. Talk about a radical new product inspired by current trends. This was the first integration of electronics into a backpack. By listening to the marketplace and by observing the ever-increasing use of portable audio devices, we envisioned a synergy of electronics and a backpack bundled together.

In 2004, we came to the market with the iPod program. Even before the massive explosion of Apple's iPod, we got a conversation going with Apple's design people. We told them we understood how big their portable music player would be and explored how JanSport could link the two brands that kids wanted to identify with—JanSport and Apple. They caught the vision and we got to work.

The second generation of the LiveWire pack featured an externally mounted five-button control strip which allows the user to operate their iPod while the iPod remains safely tucked away inside the pack. We tossed in some cool Blue Tooth connectivity which actually synchronizes the use of an iPod with a cell phone and an answering mechanism.

Here's how this works. Let's say your hiking, or skiing, or just riding the bus with your pack and you're listening to your iPod. And, let's say you have a phone call coming in. A few years ago, you'd have to pause the iPod, take off your headphones, fish your cell phone out of a purse or a pocket, answer the call, return the phone to its place, put the ear buds back into your ears, and then hit play on your iPod. Talk about old school.

But with our innovative design, all you need is the simple touch of a certain button on the pack's shoulder strap, which pauses the music and automatically switches you to your cell phone. What's more, you just talk to a speaker that's built into the shoulder strap itself. You hear the call through your headphones that you already have on. It's like listening to whoever you're talking to on the phone in stereo. Once you hang up the call, you touch a button on the strap and go right back to your iPod music. The whole experience is seamless.

But we didn't stop there.

I'm a people watcher. I've made a habit of observing how people function, what they carry, how they juggle their stuff, and what they wear. At the front end of the iPod craze, I noticed how impractical carrying an iPod was given all the other things people

167

tote around. It dawned on me that you needed something to carry your iPod in (if you're not traveling with a pack) because you're not going to hold it in your hand necessarily at all times, especially if you also have a cell phone or Palm Pilot-type device. We talked about this at JanSport and thought it would be cool if we made a specific spot for the iPod inside of a jacket.

Because of our experience with the LiveWire product, we wanted to take the technology which we had used in our packs and add it to our garments while specifically serving the iPod crowd. While we were not the only manufacturers who saw the potential of a jacket pre-wired for use with the iPod, we were the first pack and apparel company to come out with a mass offering.

Our solution? We added the same integrated functionality of our packs to our line of outer jackets. A cool control strip located just above the left front pocket on the jacket allows the wearer to switch between his or her favorite iPod tune and cell phone as needed. What's more, these jackets are washable. We surround all of the electronics in an impregnated PU layer. Just like our packs, if you're out in the rain, there's no issue with it being wet. Both are weather resistant.

I bet Captain America wishes he had had that option while cruising across the country.

THE LIFE OF THE PARTY

Designs such as the ones I'm describing are always a collaborative effort at JanSport. Everyone on our team has some sort of input. From our sales reps and designers to our customer service people, we listen to the suggestions they make. Sure I've got a lot of my own ideas, but to succeed in this business you've got to be a sponge.

Here's a perfect example of an idea for an innovative product which emerged from the team. We know that the majority of our business is the back-to-school student. We also know people are carrying stuff all year-round. Kids are going to the beach or a ball game. They're camping or they're going someplace and spending a lot of time with friends or family in the summertime. And we know that music will be a big part of their outdoor experience. So, we wanted to create something that would be fun to carry that was not necessarily a "book bag" and that incorporated music. We tossed that idea out to the team to brainstorm.

We decided to combine three things—a cooler, a stereo, and a backpack—and marry them with some of our new LiveWire technologies. At the same time, we wanted to have enough space inside the bag to throw in a couple of towels. It had to be waterproof and relatively shockproof. Talk about a tall order! And yet, our folks rose to the challenge.

For the Spring of '06, we incorporated a flat-panel speaker into a compression-molded panel mounted on the inside of a weatherproof pack and linked that with our five-button iPod controller. Now kids can broadcast the music from their iPod (managed through the shoulder straps) much like a stereo, while lying on the beach. We added what's called a Lo-Jac connection so if they wanted to clip in and use just their ear buds and not share the music with everyone, they could do that as well.

Then, we put a cooler into the base of the pack so they can hold and keep cold a 12-pack of beverages for the beach or other outdoor activities. We built in a little over 2,100 cubic inches of storage capacity, which is quite a bit of space. Best of all, it's so well made, they could drop the pack from ten feet up in the air and it wouldn't affect the speaker or the cooler. Once again, our team developed a cool product that has become one hot item.

The bottom line is that it pays to pay attention to the trends of the culture not simply to be "trendy," but to meet the ever-changing needs. Those who are unwilling to go with the flow are sure to miss the boat. Which is why as the times keep a-changin', JanSport is right there adding fun and fashion to the function of our gear . . . whether or not you're still wearing bell bottoms.

Skip in Bhutanese wardrobe. Photo by Winnie Kingsbury.

16

YKK ZIPPER CAMP

*T*he wind howled like a horde of hungry coyotes. At 10,000 feet, it was our ninth day in the same socks, but no matter. We trudged on. We were flat-footed zombies, fueled by handfuls of gorp (the fancy name for trail mix) and the desire to test what our newest packs were made of. The year? Anytime between 1967 and last month. The place? One of the high ridges, wilderness ranges, or backcountry sites where people eat things like reconstituted chili or Army surplus beef jerky . . . and chase it with a hearty belch.

We were out tramping around in our natural habitat, testing JanSport's latest pack innovations, what we liked to call "conducting research and product development" in the great outdoors. I mean, do you think a big idea like the flexible aluminum frame came from sitting around in a cubical listening to Muzak? No way. It comes from being out *there.*

If you think perfecting the perfect backpack is easy, I assure you it's not. Try spending four days with a stiff, welded pack rubbing you in all of the wrong places on your shoulders and back. Toss in a few sleepless nights in the tent to think about the chaffing, raw flesh that stings worse than a hive of agitated yellow jackets. Pretty soon you'll dream of a better pack, one without welded parts or rigid joints. And you'll see visions of a flexible frame that allows a load to move with the body. At least that's the way the process works for us.

You see, we want our customers to fall in love with their packs, which is why we put our gear through every performance challenge imaginable. The same technology, great materials, and solid construction that we use for the mountaineer is incorporated into the daypack that a student drags around 365 days of the year, often times mud and rain and water. We make JanSport products so rugged and durable, they'll always comes through for the customer. This is why since 1970, JanSport bookbags and daypacks have been *the* favorite choice of students, day hikers, and those business renegades who refuse to carry a briefcase.

Since the beginning, we've been purveyors of quality. That might sound like a slogan, but it's our way of doing business. Early on, we figured we could make packs with inferior materials in order to save a few pennies and maximize short-term profits. Even without an MBA from Harvard, we knew using second-rate components would cause the packs to fall apart in no time. Ultimately, we'd spend long, boring hours answering hate mail. No thanks.

On the other hand, we could make the best possible pack that made the customer a happy camper—as it were—in which case we wouldn't waste our afternoons digging through a mountain of complaints. According to my calculations, using nothing but top quality materials would have a long-term payoff and still leave me plenty of time to work on my tan.

JanSport has tremendous brand loyalty and for good reason. Once people realize what a ridiculous amount of stuff they can cram into our packs, how sturdy they are, and, most importantly, that we back their packs for life, they refuse to settle for less. Our commitment to excellence has paid off. To say that JanSport customers love their packs would be an understatement.

FOREVER YOURS

Maybe it's immodest to think that our customers are nicer and smarter than the competition. I bet even the most cynical person would have to admit that few companies get fan mail as inventive or complimentary as we receive. Take, for example, a letter from Eric of Fort Lauderdale, Florida. As you'll see, Eric digs his pack, big time. When he needed to take advantage of our lifetime warranty, instead of pounding out an insulting diatribe, he attached this bit of verse to his damaged daypack:

AN ODE TO MY TRUSTY RUCKSACK

> I found this rucksack years ago
> "How?" you ask. I just don't know.
> Since that time it's served me true,
> But now I'm sending it to you.
> I've had this pack for so, so long
> I thought I'd write a little song

About the times it held my books

About the sorry way it looks.

My JanSport's served me really well

It's held my gear through living hell

Its pocket's torn, the stitching's shot.

(It's also stained—a big red spot.)

The stitching inside needs repair

As well, it's now a bit threadbare.

You may wonder why I'd write

A poem about a rucksack trite.

It's because I've sent to you

A piece of me, a faded blue

Memory of where I've gone

Mornings when I've watched the dawn,

Sunsets grand and crisp, clear nights

Several transatlantic flights,

Snow-capped Alps and sun-soaked sands.

My bag has traveled many lands.

So please, oh please, be sure to see

My bag's returned real soon to me.

P.S. I hope this poem brought a smile

To your day so all the while

You're mending what I've often thrown

You'll care as if it were your own.

That's almost enough to bring a tear to the eye. Okay, maybe not. But it's evidence that our customers get real attached to their packs. How about this tribute from Mary of New Orleans? Her cherished pack fell out of her car while the shoulder strap remained wedged in the doorjamb. Amazed at the quality, she wrote and told us her story:

I dragged my JanSport backpack underneath a 1976 Honda Accord for a full hour at 60 mph over a dark, bumpy California state highway before realizing it was missing. As I pulled my "home away from home" from beneath the car, I was shocked. It was smoking and the front pocket was burned, but I didn't lose anything in the zipped pockets. Only my toothpaste and deodorant were a tad bit melted.

Although I lost use of the front unzipped pouch, I continued to use my trusty JanSport for a full year after that 1994 incident. I was recently given another pack—JanSport, of course—as a gift, and as I put my old one in the closet as a reminder of JanSport quality, I feel compelled to write you and share my experience. Keep up the good work.

Speaking of that durable, JanSport quality, this letter from Steve says it all. For more than three decades, Steve's Old Red Super Sack has been his trusted companion. Steve's letter captures the affinity and brand loyalty toward JanSport that has made us the industry leader for forty years. I'll let him tell the story:

I am writing you to recount the story of my red JanSport daypack, which I purchased while I was a high school student in Fort Wayne, Indiana in the early 1970s. I have used this daypack virtually every day for the past 32 years. I first started using my daypack during my last two years of high school. It continued to provide sturdy service for four years at Harvard, two years at Oxford, and three years of law school at Stanford. It is a well-traveled pack.

I began the practice of law in 1984, but found that I could not exchange my JanSport daypack for a briefcase. It is roomier, better designed, and much easier to carry. I have practiced law in Silicon Valley for the last 21 years and my daypack has accompanied me everywhere, including to client meetings and court appearances. For the last five years, I have been working for a New York law firm, and I suspect I am probably the only partner in a major "Wall Street" law firm to be toting a backpack.

I have been happily married for twenty-five years, and my JanSport daypack has still been with me for seven years more than my wife! So I really don't want to trade it in for a newer model. I would like to see what can be done to sew it up and reinforce it where necessary, refurbish or replace the shoulder straps and otherwise recondition it so that I can continue to use it for my remaining twenty or so years of legal practice.

My entire family uses JanSport backpacks, whether for school or, in the case of my wife, a small pack which serves as a more functional purse. My JanSport daypack is an old friend and I would like to give it the respect it deserves for its decades of reliable service.

JanSport's reputation for quality is so well established in the consumer's mind that we occasionally get credit for achievements that are not our own. I remember when a young Floridian college student got in touch to tell us that his roommate's pack had survived in the outdoors for over two years after being stolen. But when we called the roommate to verify the account, we were informed that the bag was actually *not* a JanSport. In fact, it was one of our competitors' packs. So, we thanked him for his time . . . and asked him not to repeat the story.

'TIL DEATH DO US PART

I find it interesting how many folks will write and observe that their pack is so well made that it will most likely outlive them. For example, Dorothy of Auburn, Kansas, purchased a backpack in 1998. In the fall of 2005, after traveling to a host of different countries around the world, she experienced a broken zipper. Rather than toss it, she sent it to us for repairs. She was so pleased with our service she wrote:

177

> I'm so tickled that you repaired the zipper, fixed the shoulder pads, and apparently dry cleaned it! At first, I thought you had replaced it with a brand new backpack— it was THAT GREAT!! I'll get on a soapbox and tell everyone that JanSport stands behind their products and gives great service. I may be fifty years old, but I think that my backpack will outlive me. You've made a believer out of me.

Seasoned citizen Jim sent us his Super Sack for repair and, upon receiving it back, sent us this note: "Thank you very much for replacing the two zippers. The pack has a lot of hiking miles and has been on many, many work parties maintaining the Pacific Crest Trail. I'll be 87 in a couple of months and I am sure the JanSport pack will outlast me."

I think that's so beautiful to be pushing 90 years old and to still enjoy hiking and getting under the sun. That's what it's all about. And for JanSport to play a role in Jim's outdoor experience is personally gratifying. I believe what has helped build the JanSport brand loyalty with customers like Jim has been our commitment to old-fashioned value and the fact that we really do stand behind what we make. When folks see a JanSport product in the store, they know it will last them for a lifetime, and they have confidence that we will always take good care of them should a problem develop.

If people are unhappy with a product's quality, they're not going to have a warm, fuzzy feeling about that brand. In turn, they're going to tell ten other people that they have had a bad experience. In the long run, you're not only affected by the loss of that customer, you're also affected by the other people that they tell. I stand amazed at how many businesses today fail to grasp that simple concept.

No wonder customers tend to have an elevated level of skepticism when a company claims to stand behind their products. For instance, Bill is a 55-year-old Federal retiree. Ten years ago, his son gave him a JanSport backpack. The stitching holding one of the shoulder straps to the pack was coming loose. Although he remembered our lifetime warranty, his confidence that we'd make good on our pledge was as frayed as his pack's strap. Thankfully, he decided to see what we were made of and took us up on our service guarantee. He writes:

178

To be honest, I was skeptical that the "lifetime warranty" would be honored. As you know, there are many companies that do not backup their warranty claims as they should. I shipped my pack to your facility and, to my delight, received it back the following week with the strap repaired as good as new. I was further pleasantly surprised to receive a card from your facility apologizing to me for the loss of use of my pack while it was being repaired.

Your company's actions demonstrated outstanding customer service! My pack was repaired fully and promptly, at no charge to me, and you even took the trouble to write to me and apologize for the brief time it took to make the repair. I'm very impressed with your products, your warranty, your repairs, and your customer service.

179

A company's service will only be as good as the people they employ. In our case, JanSport has benefited by having two long time staffers, Renee Fox and Robyn Kibby, at the helm of our warranty service department. For almost thirty years, these faithful employees have used their product knowledge, their experience, and their wonderful smiles to serve our customers with excellence.

Without question, providing superior products and exceptional customer service are two ways JanSport has retained its stellar reputation. But as a company, we're also known for creating good vibrations along the way. As I've said, one of our company's core principles is that we'll make fun a part of everything we do. But how could we make the repair process fun for the customer? Try this on for size . . .

POSTCARDS FROM YKK ZIPPER CAMP

If you're like most people, you probably could tell me a customer service horror story when attempting to submit an item for repair at a local merchant. We've all had them. I'm not sure when the prevailing business trend started to move away from providing good customer service. That change is just bad for business, which is why we wanted to be different. We at JanSport wanted the customer care experience to be both pleasant and memorable—in a good way. That's why when our warranty department receives a daypack or backpack with a damaged zipper, we thought it would be a fun idea to mail its owner a postcard with the following message:

Hi! It's me, your favorite Back Pack.

Warranty Service Camp is really cool. The other packs are really different, and I love my pack counselor. I miss hanging out with you and carrying your gear all the time. I can't wait to see you! They say they're sending me home soon. Gotta run . . . we're doing zipper races today!

Signed, Little Pack

JANSPORT

Hi, Pack Owner!

I'm your pack's Warranty Service Camp counselor, Big J.S. I really enjoyed getting to know Little J.S., whom you must desperately, at camp this year. Of course the little rascal than a few problems, so we got to work right away. We thing, but Little J.S. just couldn't be restored to full zipp

To cheer you up, please adopt this strapping new pack Lifetime Warranty Program.

Every Happiness,
Big J.S.

Jan Lewis
JanSport Cofounder - 1967

Replace

JANSPORT

Hi, Pack Owner!

I'm your pack's counselor, Big J.S. We really enjoyed getting to know little J.S. at Warranty Service Camp this year – what a star! A strapping little rascal, your pack led the pack in bug smashing, carrying ghost stories, and as you know, Little J.S. made quite a showing in the zipper races.

We know you must have missed the little bagger like crazy. You'll be pleased to know that we worked out those little problems that you told us about, so your pack is back to full zip strength.

Every happiness,
Big J.S.

Repair

Jan Lewis
JanSport Cofounder - 1967

Repair reply cards

Then, when we ship the repaired pack back to its owner, we enclose this postcard from Zipper Camp:

Hi Pack Owner!

I'm your pack's counselor, Big J.S. We really enjoyed getting to know little J.S. at Warranty Service Camp this year—what a star! A strapping little rascal, your pack led the pack in bug smashing, carrying ghost stories, and as you know, Little J.S. made quite a showing in the zipper races. We know you must have missed the little bagger like crazy. You'll be pleased to know that we worked out those little problems that you told us about, so your pack is back to full zip strength.

Every happiness,

Signed, Big J.S.

People absolutely love that personal touch. First, we informed them that we'd received their pack and then we told them when to expect it back. By taking that extra step in customer service, we answer a lot of questions and save them from the hassle of calling. And, we served it up in a fun way that resonates with them. I can't tell you how many times in my travels people say, "Skip, I sent in my pack and got this really great card back about my pack being at camp."

To be honest, the zippers on our packs rarely need servicing because for thirty-nine years, we've used the YKK brand zipper. YKK is a superior product made of nylon coils, whereas many of the zippers used in the early days were brass zippers which would freeze up, lock up, or jam. Thanks to the innovation and reliability of the YKK zipper, our packs have enjoyed a minimum of zipper-related failures. The YKK zipper is so good, often times when a customer sends in a pack to have the zipper fixed, the zipper didn't fail. The damage was through abuse or misuse.

Nevertheless, in many of those cases we make the repair in order to keep the customer happy. Sending a postcard is just another way to make their repair experience enjoyable. Believe it or not, some people have actually written back to their pack counselor. Take, for instance, customer Nancy. She was so pleased with our service that she helped her daypack write a note of its own:

Dear Warranty Service Camp Director,

Thanks for a great stint at camp. I really liked my pack counselor and had a great time with the zipper race. I got so good at it that my owner says I'm zipping around better than ever! She's so happy to have me home that she's letting me carry her gear again. Say "Hi" to the other packs for me!

Thanks again for everything!

Signed, Little Pack

People love to tell us stories about their JanSport pack or product. Those stories are inspired because of our commitment to maintaining the highest standards and treating each customer with the utmost respect. Which means, when they tell us about a problem, it's not going to be a problem for us.

GIVING BACK AND FUNDRAISER FUN

As a young man growing up in Great Bend, Kansas, I loved playing baseball. I loved everything about the game. From the smell of my freshly oiled leather glove to the crack of the bat while shagging flies, baseball gave me such joy. I couldn't wait for summer so my friends and I could play ball. Knowing my love of the game, my folks encouraged me to join the local Little League baseball team. I signed up on the first day and was quickly identified as the pitcher. In the games when I wasn't scheduled to pitch, I played any number of positions in the infield.

Years later when I was in high school, the Director of Recreation came to me and said, "Skip, we've got a Little League team and none of the fathers want to coach these younger boys. Would you consider stepping up to the plate for them and be their coach?" Keep in mind I was a high school-aged boy and had no previous coaching experience. All the same, I was honored that he would ask. I told him I'd be happy to coach that team.

As I would later learn, the young boys in question were from a lower class part of town—the poor families from the wrong side of the tracks. When I was first introduced, the faces staring back at me were Hispanics, African Americans, and some Caucasians. As I worked with them, I quickly found that many had a natural talent for the sport. They were born to be athletes. All they needed was a little coaching and mentoring to become great. Indeed, they did. We won most of our games because of their inherent skill.

Looking back, I could see how an investment in their lives made all of the difference in the world regarding their future success. With each win, the boys scored a fresh dose of self-confidence. They learned the value of teamwork and, most importantly, how to handle defeat with honor after the rare lost game. For my part, the experience was a homerun. I felt a deep

184

Skip (center row, far right) and the Park Dodgers of Great Bend, Kansas.
Photo by Great Bend Daily Tribune.

satisfaction from giving of myself to serve others who were less fortunate.

In the grand scheme of things, my stint as a Little League coach in Kansas would set the stage for JanSport to give back to "at risk" youth years later. As I would soon learn, the mountains these young people faced were measured in terms of gang influence, violence, crime, poverty, and broken households. If I could harness my position as a businessman to reach even one troubled teen, that would make it all worthwhile for me. As it turns out, JanSport was able to reach many more than just one.

BIG CITY MOUNTAINEERS

Back in the 1980s, I was walking the convention floor at the Outdoor Retailer tradeshow in Reno, Nevada. A gentleman named Jim Kern approached and asked me if he could have a couple minutes of my time. If you've ever been to an outdoor convention, the place is busier than a beehive before winter. It's literally swarming with people networking and buying or selling goods and services. Because of my role at JanSport, I usually can only walk about ten feet before an old friend, a potential customer, or a vender will stop me.

Furthermore, my personal philosophy has been to treat each person I meet with dignity and respect. So, even though I had no idea who this man was or what he wanted, we pulled aside and sat down at a table to talk. Jim promised not to take too much of my time as he pulled out a book. Thumbing through page after page of pictures, he said, "Skip, I have a non-profit program called Big City Mountaineers (BCM) where I take kids into the outdoors and give them an experience of a lifetime. These are kids that have been in trouble, sometimes with the law. Many have been in court-ordered youth group centers. We host a couple of outdoor hiking trips every year in Colorado and sometimes in Utah. I'm really struggling to provide frame packs for these kids. They don't have packs. Is there anything JanSport can do to help us help these kids?"

Something in my heart resonated with what Jim was describing. I'm sure somewhere in the back of my mind, my work with the Little League team back in Kansas affirmed the value of standing with those who need a break. I said, "Sure, we'll get you a dozen packs that are appropriate for the kids." Jim was so grateful for the much needed assistance.

The next year, BCM gave us a report highlighting what had happened with some of the youth. They then requested additional gear to expand their program. We welcomed the chance to work with them again and, for several years, provided more gear. Then, one day, a new thought came to me. JanSport works with a lot of youth—in the sense that young people use our products. So, wouldn't it be cool if we took a regular portion of our company profits and gave back to specific causes that helped troubled teens?

I approached the officers of our committee that handles our non-profit giving, Paul Delorey, Harv Erickson, Mike Cisler, Jim Koehne, and Karin Apitz. They agreed it would be really cool if we helped fund a group that was working with "at risk" youth. I called Jim Kern, the founder of BCM, and said, "You know, Jim, if you really want to do something big, why don't you come up and give us a big pitch?"

We were aware of the work of BCM, having supplied them with packs for several years. We also knew that Jim had been the founder of other worthy groups, including the Florida Trails Association and the American Hiking Society. Jim came to our headquarters and gave us a great presentation. I think we blew his socks off when we told him that we wanted to get involved with a sizeable donation. We also asked to put a couple of people on their board of directors to assist them in future fundraising efforts.

I was invited to become one of the BCM board members and am pleased to report that JanSport is still very involved as a financial contributor and supplier of equipment. My title with Big City Mountaineers is Vice President of Industry Relations and I was appointed to serve for two terms on their executive committee.

Our involvement has included more than lending our name and finances to their worthy cause. I have personally been on a number of BCM trips with a group of boys. It's probably one of the more gratifying things I do. In my view, investing in a teenager's life is like throwing a stone into a pond. If you can affect the life of one kid over the course of a week in the mountains, the ripples of that time spent will resonate throughout the rest of his or her life.

Many of these youth have never been to a lake or a mountain. We start by teaching them basic outdoor skills and give them a goal of reaching the lake—which is a pretty rough hike through deep woods. They work together as a team of five youth and five volunteers for a solid time of one-on-one personal attention. They get to build their confidence while having clean, healthy fun. Best of all, they interact with a mentor who actually cares about their welfare. After a trip, a bond has formed within the group and often times between the camper and mentor.

Let me share two personal examples with you.

STAND BY ME

One of my earliest trips with Big City Mountaineers was a trek up to a lake that rests in the foothills of a mountain called Holy Cross, adjacent to Vail, Colorado. I was asked to mentor a teenager from Florida named Derrick. Like the four other teens traveling with their counselors, Derrick had to earn the right in his youth group to go on the trip. As is typically the case, Derrick had never done anything like this. He was completely outside his comfort zone.

Think about it. These teens are going from the concrete streets of the urban jungle to the wilderness and the untamed outdoors for four full days. Understandably, Derrick was filled with anxiety and questions. What if he gets lost? What happens if it starts to rain? Are there bathrooms? What about the bears? Will they attack and eat us? If someone gets sick, what then?

With each step, he began to settle down. He saw we were there for him no matter what—which is a big deal for those teens whose parents had abandoned them along the way. Derrick discovered he could keep pace and found that the hiking was liberating in ways he never imagined. Before long, we backpacked our way up to the lake and set up camp. There, we relaxed, swam, and taught the boys how to fly fish.

On this particular trip, Jim Williams, a master fly fisherman and Director of the University of Oregon Bookstore, was traveling with our group. He gave the boys instructions based on his years of practice and experience. They were riveted to his every move. It didn't take long for Derrick to get the hang of it. He got totally engrossed in fly fishing and couldn't get enough of the action. That evening while the rest of us were sitting by the campfire, Derrick was fishing well into the night. I had to smile when the next morning he was out on the lake before the rest of us.

Several weeks after the trip was over, Derrick sent me a letter in which he told me how he discovered a new passion. He was so committed to this new hobby, he worked extra hard to earn enough money to buy his own pole. The transformation that had come over Derrick was amazing. I decided to send him some gear to encourage him and keep him motivated. Over the years, Derrick has stayed in touch. He ended up back in high school to finish his education, and was looking forward to getting a part time job—to buy more fishing gear. Those few days of freedom and special attention gave Derrick a passion for life.

Like Derrick, fifteen-year-old Eric had experienced his share of hard knocks early in life. His parents divorced when he was a youngster, which, in some ways, was the spark that lit the fuse of poor choices. In a letter to me, Eric wrote:

> "During that time and [due to a] lack of positive role models, I started stealing from others. I would break into strangers' homes, searching for money, cigarettes, alcohol, and anything else that caught me eye. I was also very good at deciding my own schedule—which rarely included attending school."

189

Eric's grades sank to an all-time low due to his string of absentees. He also risked suspension. Eric continued:

> As a result of my actions, I was placed at Rawhide Boys Ranch. When I arrived at Rawhide I felt cool because I was at a place where *bad kids* are sent, and I decided to continue with that image of myself and not cooperate with the house parents or the regular school schedule.

I should point out that Rawhide Boys Ranch is another program that JanSport supports. Rawhide is a group home that welcomes "at risk" boys, teaches them self-respect, hard work, and the value of a disciplined life. Located on 714-acres just fifteen minutes from our Appleton, Wisconsin headquarters, Rawhide has made an incredible difference in the lives of hundreds of youth for several decades.

In 1968, NFL football legend and Green Bay Packer quarterback Bart Starr was struck by Rawhide's program. Wanting to do something special for Rawhide, Starr donated his MVP Chevrolet Corvette he won from Super Bowl II to the Boys Ranch. They, in turn, sold it as a fundraiser. Following Starr's lead, people to this day will donate their cars to Rawhide to be auctioned off to raise funds. Starr has also invested countless hours of personal time with the boys.

Getting back to Eric's letter, I was thrilled to see how his life changed for the better. I had spent several days canoeing to the Boundary Waters in northern Minnesota with Eric and several other boys and their leaders in June of 2004. Thanks to that trip, coupled with the fine work of Rawhide's mentoring program, Eric's life was turning around. He wrote:

"I also earned a higher allowance with my rank and recently used the money to buy whitening strips for my teeth, because I plan on smiling a lot more. Guess what else? While attending Starr Academy (Rawhide's private school), my grades have improved and I am now receiving A's, B's, and a few C's. Wow! I would never have imagined I could achieve this when I first came to Rawhide . . . I am so proud of myself."

Eric went on to tell me how he plans to attend college after graduation, with an eye on getting a job in Wisconsin "where I can start my career and my family." Isn't that fantastic? That's what giving back is all about.

SUMMIT FOR SOMEONE

One of the best nonprofit fundraisers for Big City Mountaineers I've experienced first hand is the Summit for Someone. Mark Godley, Executive Director of BCM, had a concept of guiding a small group of six climbers up five classic American peaks. Each climber would pay or raise $2,500 to participate in a once-in-a-lifetime trip. Participants would get to keep $1,700 worth of gear donated by twenty outdoor industry companies, while their climbing fee would be used to underwrite a week-long trip of mentoring for five at-risk urban teens through BCM. Talk about a win-win.

The original peaks targeted for the fundraiser were Mt. Whitney, Mt. Shasta, Mt. Hood, Mt. Olympus, and Mt. Rainer. Each team of six would be guided by RMI guides such as Craig Van

Hoy who summited the 8000 meter Kangchenjunga in 1989 as well as Peter Whittaker and Kurt Wedberg who guided many of our JanSport Rainier seminars.

Mark's idea was a real winner. The first year he had thirty available spots—they sold out in one hour. In 2006, all 120 spots were snapped up in two hours on a web-based signup, raising $300,000 for BCM. Jon Dorn, Executive Editor of *Backpacker* magazine, used the muscle of the media to help spread the word. Through a full page ad in *Backpacker* and in a sister Rodale magazine, *Men's Health*, Dorn gave a big boost to the effort.

Meanwhile, Ed Viesturs, America's premier high-altitude mountaineer, will serve as the 2007 Honorary Chairperson for the program. His involvement is sure to take the benefit climb to new heights. The Summit for Someone is a great example of the outdoor industry working together to support a successful nonprofit program.

SHAKE 'N' BAKE PARTY

During the late 1970s and into the early 1980s, the biggest trade show for the outdoor industry was the annual Ski Show in Las Vegas. The ski industry was growing so fast that they gave the adjacent hall to the outdoor industry, those who made hiking boots, backpacks, and other related gear. If you were an outdoors person, a dealer, or a player in the field, this show was the Mecca of all events.

In 1979, I caught wind of some interesting news. Three outdoor companies, Low Alpine, Caribou Mountaineering, and Wilderness Experience, were interested in joining forces to thank their dealers at the annual convention by throwing a giant block party. Without hesitation I told them that JanSport—the original party animal—wanted to join in the fun. After all, hippies like parties. We love music and dancing. And there's nothing quite like free food and good beer to wash it down.

I volunteered to make up the t-shirts and came up with a cool design that incorporated the logos from each of the four companies. The idea was that each company would distribute the t-shirts from their respective convention booths. While the shirts were given away free, you had to have one to attend. We held the first Shake 'N' Bake party at the Sahara Hotel and Casino and charged a modest admission to pay for the band. Even though

193

Design for a Shake 'N' Bake fundraiser party for Big City Mountaineers. Graphics by JanSport, Appleton.

there was a huge kitchen fire and a small army of fire trucks descended on the place, we partied on. That celebration was a great hit with upwards of 600 in attendance.

Afterward, for reasons I still can't quite explain, folks referred to the Shake 'N Bake as the "JanSport party." Understandably, the other guys thought that was a bit of a let down and decided not to make it a collaborative effort the following year. We just went ahead and hosted the *JanSport Shake 'N Bake* party ourselves. Each year, I'd print up a different t-shirt that doubled as an invitation to the party. As before, the shirts were available at our booth.

We'd hold the party at a local bar, restaurant, or even in a giant hotel lobby. About the same time that the Outdoor convention show split off from the Ski show to become its own event, we had to move the party outdoors. We've had musical guests from Elvin Bishop, Arlo Guthrie, and the Nitty Gritty Dirt band to the Black Eyed Peas. We've literally taken over a whole downtown city block as the event now attracts thousands of happy people.

What's this got to do with fundraising? About ten years ago, JanSport decided to tap into the goodwill that the legendary Shake 'N Bake dance party produced. We've used it as yet another vehicle to raise funds for worthy non-profit causes like Big City Mountaineers and the Outdoor Industry Association ever since.

Who said raising money has to be a drag?

SHOW ME THE MONEY

On the corporate level, we have two committees within JanSport that are assigned with the privilege of giving back to the community. That blows my mind considering the fact that when we started out, we couldn't even pay ourselves. The concept of supporting the efforts of others was simply out of our reach. But, as we have prospered, I not only believe it's the right thing to do, but that it's plain old good business to give back some of the blessing.

In our case, one committee evaluates the thousands of requests for donations and sponsorships we receive annually. As you can imagine, we have set a certain budget and the committee makes grant decisions based upon our internally set priorities. The second committee deals specifically with the non-profit companies that we have chosen to get involved with, such as Big City Mountaineers, The Continental Trail Divide Alliance, Outdoor Industry Association, the Outdoor Industry Women's Council, and the Conservation Alliance, which is a non-profit foundation that awards grants to environmentally oriented projects.

Just as we have made a commitment to give back at the corporate level, we also encourage our employees to do the same. Over the years we've had some pretty fun internal giving campaigns. For example, take the "LET'S CAN SKIP" promotion. The art department cooked up a life-sized mural of me wearing all of my mountain climbing gear walking along a snow covered ridge. This mural was about thirty to forty feet long. We invited employees to cover the mural with canned goods which we would then deliver to the Food Pantry. Employees who brought in cans got to wear a pin which proclaimed: "I CANNED SKIP."

But that's not all. Being the competitive people that we are, JanSport was competing against Kimberly-Clark, School Specialties, and other select companies across town to see who could solicit the most cans. I'm not surprised that JanSport won the food drive with the most number of cans . . . for three years in a row. The first year we generated 14,000 cans. The next year, 55,000 cans covered the mural. The third year we topped 65,000 cans.

Another program that gave our employees a chance to give back to the community was the Families of Freedom Scholarship Fund, which provided money for college for the children whose parents had been killed in the 9/11 attacks on the Twin Towers, the Pentagon, and United Flight 93. JanSport employees raised a total of $62,000 using food drives, car washes, bake sales, and a host of creative approaches to raising money.

JanSport also got heavily involved in a climb to raise funds to fight breast cancer. The goal was $2.1 million and was tied into a climb of South America's Aconcagua Mountain. The team was comprised of women who were survivors of breast cancer, including Laura Evans who had attended a JanSport dealer climb in previous years. Peter Whittaker, Lou's son, was the team leader of the climb. For a full year, we helped promote that effort and helped raise the full amount. That's a good example of using mountain climbing as a tool to bring awareness to a worthy cause while raising money.

While some of the promotions were conducted on a large scale, such as the Aconcagua climb, many were smaller, individual efforts. For instance, when Dennis Judkins, a long time employee, organized a walk for juvenile diabetes, JanSport provided the t-shirts.

In another effort, JanSport president Paul DeLorey (now retired) and Michael Wenger pulled together a band called Rickey Lee and the Pretenders that played on Fridays with an open guitar case for money for charity. Paul even arranged a pie throw-

Peggy McNally and Skip posing for a "Hold on to Summer" promotion.

ing contest; several key leaders were picked to be "pied." The employee who donated the most money got the chance to throw a pie in the face of one of the executives. That was always a crowd pleaser.

One of the core principles of JanSport is that we believe there's more to life than a day's work. Just punching a time clock is so old school. But getting involved beyond the office walls with real life opportunities to provide for those in need has its own rewards.

If it's not abundantly clear already, we believe in taking the same energy we use to sell stuff to do good for other people in the community. If JanSport is going to have a food drive for the needy, we don't want to just have a food drive. We want to get the most food they ever saw. In that respect, we'll always play to win. If somebody needs help or is in trouble, we don't want to do a minimal job. We'll go the extra mile. As it's been said, it's better to give than to receive.

Why am I so big on giving back? There's a certain personal satisfaction and joy that comes from nurturing a generous spirit or, put another way, an attitude of gratitude. But I've always believed that if you do the right thing toward others *because it's the right thing to do*, you'll never need to engage in artificial public relations.

Giving back is not only good for the soul, it's good for business.

197

REACH OUT AND TOUCH SOMEONE

While there are many non-profit organizations worthy of your support, here are the links to those I've mentioned in this chapter. Whether you want to partner with one of these fine organizations or with another group, the real fun and personal satisfaction begins when you see lives changed through your participation.

Outdoor Industry Association (www.outdoorindustry.org)

Conservation Alliance (www.conservationalliance.com)

Continental Divide Trail Alliance (www.cdtrail.org)

Outdoor Industry Women's Council (www.oiwc.org)

Big City Mountaineers (www.bigcitymountaineers.org)

GET OUT WHILE YOU CAN

I've never been the president of JanSport. Does that come as a shock? Think about it. I've written a book about climbing the corporate ladder and yet I stopped one rung short of the top slot. More baffling to some is the fact that Murray and Jan have left JanSport to charter new pathways of their own. Murray left JanSport in 1982 to pursue other interests. Jan stayed on with the company for several decades and retired in the fall of 2005. That makes me the last of the three co-founders still having fun and kicking up trouble around the office. Why, then, has the president's office remained outside of my reach? That's easy.

Planting a flag on the pinnacle of JanSport's corporate hill has never been the aspiration of this mountain climbing hippie. I happen to enjoy the view from my perch as the Vice President of Global Public Relations. In this capacity, I get to travel and stay connected with the cast of characters I've befriended over four decades. And there's still plenty of time to meet and make new friendships while serving the company that I love. Presidents have to plow through piles of paperwork. Now, honestly, which role would you choose?

This might be the most important lesson of all: *Quit climbing once you've found your "sweet spot."* Anything beyond that point is like lugging excess baggage. Many aspiring business-types strive to become the Top Dog, the Head Honcho, or the Big Cheese. There's nothing inherently wrong with that. But if in your pursuit of the corner office, you discover that your true passion lies midway up the corporate ladder, stop climbing and enjoy what you've found!

Here's a personal example.

I've loved popcorn ever since I was a kid. When I was young, I was the first to volunteer to make the family popcorn. I loved playing around in the kitchen trying to perfect the cooking process. Admittedly, I'd always give myself a big bowl and then everybody would get a regular-sized one. As an adult, I researched a wide range of popping corn from organic to imported. Ultimately, I started to grow my own popcorn as a hobby. Just for the fun of it, I launched a private label of unpopped gourmet popcorn called, "Howlin' Yowelln' Himalayan Popcorn." Whenever I'd host a seminar, I'd give out free samples.

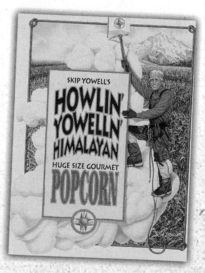

As you might guess, there were those who loved my popcorn and asked if I had plans to start a small company. Actually, there was a period of time when I did just that. But it wasn't long before I put the break-even endeavor on the shelf. Why? I didn't possess the inner fire to take it to the next level. When the pleasure that my hobby originally produced started to ebb and when the work offered more hassles than rewards, I knew it was time to let it go.

With JanSport, however, each new day brings with it an opportunity to build on the legacy that started in my uncle's transmission shop. To this day, I genuinely enjoy the people on our team. I'm energized by the freedom I have to help the next generation of JanSport employees catch the vision, push the boundaries of discovery, and bend a few of the rules of decorum just for laughs. When it comes to my corporate climb, then, I've found my sweet spot. Truthfully, I can't imagine topping what I've experienced along the way. On second thought, dinner with Dylan would be way beyond cool.

As long as I'm on a reflective vibe, one of the most gratifying aspects of my work has been to serve on the board of the Outdoor Industry Association (OIA). Interestingly, we were originally named the Outdoor Recreation Coalition of America (ORCA) when founded in 1989. However, our initials, ORCA, just happened to spell the name of a killer whale. Initially people were confused. They thought we were a fish-related advocacy firm. So, several years ago, I helped orchestrate the name change in order to reposition us in the market. Nothing against fish. Our scope just happens to be broader. And today, OIA has grown to provide trade services to 4,000 like-minded Outdoor Industry-oriented retailers, suppliers, distributors, manufacturers, and sales representatives. That's a mouthful.

What it means is that a cross-section of national and regional companies joined hands to make a difference in all aspects of promoting the outdoor lifestyle. Through seminars, conventions, advocacy, and benefit events for non-profit partners, OIA has become an indispensable ally of the adventure-minded soul.

Although competitors on one level, OIA members came to see that there was real value in speaking with a unified voice about the issues that are important to all of us. From fostering wilderness conservation and providing industry research, to government affairs and consumer outreach, OIA has become the "go to" source whenever the media or perhaps an outdoor enthusiast seeks information in our field of expertise. We've also promoted the notion that the wilderness is a sacred gift worthy of our enjoyment, protection, and conservation.

Plainly put, just as there's a right and a wrong way to have fun, there's a right and wrong way to engage in outdoor recreation. Allow me to dip into the oldies file and dig out a personal example.

WALK ON THE WILD SIDE

The early days of JanSport got a little insane at times. I'm talking we had pedal-to-the-medal, premium-octane fun. We were known in the industry as the "wild bunch" because we out-danced, out-partied, and outdid every competitor we ever laid eyes on. For the most part, the merrymaking and cavorting was nothing more than innocent fun. On occasion, we danced our way over the edge. Now that the Sixties haze has worn off, I can see more clearly and recognize our missteps.

Many years ago, we were hosting a JanSport tradeshow booth at the annual Ski Show in Las Vegas. One of our reps made arrangements for us to stay at The Jockey Club resort. This was one of those upscale places with marble everywhere. You might say it was a real classy joint—certainly nicer than most of our usual digs on the road. All of our sales reps and management team were booked into the facility.

Coincidently, one of the JanSport marketing managers, Bob Shaw, was getting married at the time. About ten of us decided to throw Bob a bachelor party—JanSport style. Not far from the hotel was a club featuring a B-level comedian. After quite a few beers, John Andreas and Walt Mullen, one of the reps, and a couple of the guys in our group ended up heckling the comedian. Frankly, they were much funnier than the comedian. The manager, however, wasn't laughing, and he promptly threw us out.

We arrived back at the Jockey Club hotel around 3:30 in the morning and took the elevator up to the fourth floor. Being in a rowdy frame of mind, we thought it would be fun to hose down Craig Perpich, one of our sales managers, while he was sleeping. At least we *assumed* that Craig was already asleep in his room because he was too tired to participate in the bachelor party.

When we got off of the elevator we noticed a fire hose conveniently mounted on the wall. I started to turn the wheel to activate the water while Walt and John started unreeling the hose down the hall. Since John was sharing the room with Craig, he had a key to get in. About halfway down the hall, the pressure finally hit the end of the hose and the thing started twirling around yanking itself out of Walt and John's hands.

At that point, I just took off and went up a flight of stairs to my room. Meanwhile, as I would later learn, John grabbed the hose and scrambled to his room wrestling for control of the hose the whole way. Unfortunately, Craig wasn't in the room. At that point, I'm not exactly sure why somebody didn't turn the hose off. Instead, Walt, John, and the others let the water run for several hours until it started to cascade down the stairwell like a waterfall . . . and the water seeped into various rooms along the way. I didn't have a clue this was happening.

Craig was out all night and returned to the hotel at 6:00 in the morning. When he got off the elevator, he saw water pouring everywhere—it had been gushing for almost three hours at that point. Craig sloshed his way to his room and called down to the front desk to alert them of the problem. I'm not sure how this flood didn't come to their attention sooner. Nevertheless, a bellman came and turned off the fire hose. Craig had no earthly idea that we were the ones who had turned it on in the first place.

The next morning, I came down for a quick breakfast and then went over to work in our booth on the convention floor. I was the first to arrive, still unaware of the flood that had ensued in my absence. Suddenly, I saw a number of really big guys coming directly towards me shaking their heads. Moments later, they stepped into our booth and, standing real close to me, said, "There's big time trouble, pal. Water got into a bunch of the rooms. And you know what? Buddy isn't happy." That got my attention.

Buddy Rose was the hotel manager and, frankly, looked a lot like a New Jersey hit man straight out of HBO's hit show *The Sopranos*. They studied my face with a glare. After a long, highly uncomfortable minute, they told me that Buddy wanted to see me in his office. "And another thing," one of them croaked, "Buddy wants to remind you how close Lake Meade is—you better not leave town without paying for all of your fun."

By now, John and Walt had arrived. I gave them a heads-up and, after a quick pow-wow, we decided we had to do the right thing and confess we were the ones who did it. That wasn't an easy decision to make. We were imagining figures of $8,000 in damages. John and his wife were on the verge of having their first child. I had just bought a house and placed a big down payment on it. I was stretched to the limit. The last thing we needed was a big bill like that.

But what's fair is fair. We went back to the hotel to pay the piper. We went to the front desk and asked to see Buddy Rose. We were told he was busy but to go sit down in the restaurant and wait. It was still relatively early and there was virtually nobody around. We took a seat and waited . . . the whole time hammering out our story.

When Buddy finally marched in, my stomach started doing back flips. He didn't sit down. Raising an eyebrow, he said, "I hear you guys want to talk to me."

I managed a smile. "You know that little problem you had last night with the water? We were the guys responsible."

Buddy crossed his arms. "Yea, I got the sheriff's department up there fingerprinting. You wouldn't have been able to leave town. We'd have caught you."

Police? This was not good news.

Buddy said, "Look, I was young once. I'll make you a deal. You just have to pay the damages—today. I'll know what they are in about an hour. I'll call you into my office." With that, he turned and left us to ponder our fate. For the next forty-five minutes,

John and I were trying to figure out what we were going to do. Buddy had said that we weren't going to leave town until the damages were paid for. How could we put our hands on upwards of $8,000?

I kept picturing Lake Meade and started to wonder how many bodies were at the bottom wearing a pair of concrete shoes.

We were finally summoned into Buddy's office, obviously pretty shook up about the consequences. Buddy sat behind a giant desk and pointed to the two chairs in front of him. As we sat, he slid a sheet of paper toward us. I stole a glance at John and then looked at the page. Buddy said, "Boy, I don't believe it. The charges are going to be $800."

Truly, that was the greatest news I ever heard. I tried to hide my enthusiasm. We asked if we could put it on our American Express cards. He agreed and we asked him to split the bill and to put it under "Housecleaning." We thanked Buddy, paid the bill, and left. Every year, for a couple of years thereafter, I invited Buddy to a big dinner that JanSport sponsored. Interestingly, we became friends. As it turns out, Buddy was into hiking so I made sure he had plenty of JanSport gear. I never confessed that we thought it was going to be a whole lot more than $800, although now he'll know the rest of the story.

Here's the connection to my work at OIA: There's a right and a wrong way to have fun. Mistakes happen. Sometimes the craziness gets out of hand, as it did in this situation. When it does, it's up to each person to do the right thing, own up to it, and correct the damage—especially when a prank, an accident, or poor judgment impacts other people or the great outdoors.

That's why our efforts at OIA in the area of the stewardship and conservation of our national parks and public wilderness areas are so vital. Natural areas should be enjoyed but preserved. One way is to practice a "leave nothing behind" attitude. In other words, when you camp, boat, hike, or climb, be sure to bring out everything you bring in. And, at the risk of sounding like Smokey the Bear's first cousin, use care when building and extinguishing a campfire.

As you and I care for the planet—even in small ways like refusing to litter—we will preserve the environment that will serve us well for decades to come. So, get outdoors as often as you can. Have a blast. Be responsible. And, as we used to say in the Sixties, "Love Your Mother Earth."

THE LONG AND WINDING ROAD

We have reached the end of the journey.

I have no illusions about what this book may have done for you. I sincerely doubt you will be a better mountain climber as a consequence of lingering on the trail with me. After all, this wasn't a "how to" manual. Nor can I say with any degree of certainty that you'll be the next industrious soul to ascend the lofty heights of the corporate ladder where Bill Gates, Donald Trump, and other business tycoons dwell.

If I've done anything of lasting value, I hope it will have been this: that you will heed the call to explore this amazing planet and, in turn, find the hidden treasures that await your discovery; that you will love and have fun with your work—if not, that you'll stop, change course, and pursue the passions of your soul; and that JanSport's example of a commitment to excellence, value, and innovation will continue to inspire you reach your goals, regardless of the mountain you choose to climb.

Forty years ago, we had a vision to make quality outdoor gear hip and innovative and we wanted to have fun doing it. On that note, I can safely say, mission accomplished.

It's appropriate, then, to thank you for making JanSport the global leader in our field. Without you, Murray, Jan, and I wouldn't have had the chance to chase our dreams, see the world, meet so many cool people—and have more fun than most folks could imagine. What more could a hippie ask for?

Now, isn't it time you blazed your own trail?

Skip in New Zealand on the Milford Track: The finest walk in the world.

ACKNOWLEDGEMENTS

As I set out to write this book, I was faced with the fact that there are many stories and adventures to tell. Each one has been special. One of my most favorite trips, for example, was climbing Mt. Kilimanjaro, the highest peak in Africa. Lou and Ingrid Whittaker, Peter and Eric Whittaker, several friends, Jan Lewis, and I spent seven days in the Masai Mara Wildlife Preserve in Kenya viewing the exotic animals—a very exciting experience. I felt as if I had been transported into the movie, *Out of Africa*.

We climbed to the summit of Kilimanjaro starting in the far end of the jungle and then traversed down the standard route. We finished off the trip on the coast of Africa at Mombassa, enjoying the beaches, water, food, and cultures. Each summit brings with it a feeling of joy, accomplishment, and personal reward of success. Mountain climbing, however, is not just about reaching the summit. It's also about the travels to and from, as well as the

209

cultures and people you meet and experience along the way that makes the journey worthwhile.

The same can be said about writing a book. These pages wouldn't exist if it were not for the special friends, family members, and fellow travelers who filled forty years with more stories than this book can contain.

Murray McCory, my talented cousin; Jan Lewis, such a wonderful, dedicated mother, and a very key part of building the JanSport brand. Lou Whittaker, a teacher and mentor supreme, is a key individual in JanSport brand building. Lou, his wife, Ingrid, and I experienced so many great trips and adventures together.

Paul DeLorey has an unmatched style of leadership and carried the JanSport banner with style.

The family who have all been involved and contributed include Aunt Mabel Newman and the Pletz family, my sister Diana, brothers Randy and Lindsey Yowell, and Mom and Dad, who have a special place in our hearts. Thanks also to Heidi Van Brost, Joy Robison, Lynn Yowell, Lindsey Yowell, Jr.

Peter Jenkins, a great friend and fellow adventurer, was an advisor to me on this book.

I'd also like to thank Thomas Nelson Publishing for having faith in my story, and Rebekah Whitlock of NAKED INK, who made this all possible and contributed so many great ideas.

JanSport employees of the past and the present have contributed so many great ideas. To the JanSport sales reps of the past and present who have contributed and made this story possible, I thank them deeply.

To the many vendors and retailers, I have appreciated their support and friendship over the years.

ACKNOWLEDGEMENTS

Thanks to Peter Whittaker and the great Rainier Mountaineers Inc. (RMI) guides who have led our seminars over the years and the fun factor they have provided.

The VF Corporation, who has been a great parent company since 1986, provided the JanSport brand with great tools and leadership and special attention from Mackey MacDonald, Eric Wiseman, Dan Templin and Bob Shearer of VF.

The JanSport teams in Everett, WA; Appleton, WI; San Leandro, CA; Brussels, Belgium, VF Hong Kong are made up of great groups of people, and a fun leader, Mike Corvino will take the brand to new levels.

To Bob DeMoss whom I collaborated with on this story, I greatly appreciate all of his creative skills.

Thank you to my great office support of Peggy McNally in Appleton, Wisconsin and Melissa Vogel in San Leandro, California for her transcribing of the book.

I'd also like to recognize the very talented equipment sales reps as well as the incredible staff for their dedication and hard work at the non profits of Outdoor Industry Association and Big City Mountaineers, plus the hardworking board members of each group.

Thank you to the millions of loyal consumers who have chosen JanSport products over the past 40 years.

To my longtime childhood friends Dannis Robison, Dan Anderson, John Lytle, and Paul Folds—each worked or contributed in his own way to my journey.

My wonderful wife, Winnie Kingsbury, has supported me every step of the way, as did Bean, Wesley, and Drew Kingsbury.

My precious daughter, Quinn, has many years of adventure ahead and a great understanding of our environment.

211

I'd like to thank Keith Roush for his dedication and contributions.

Amber Brookman, Bob Stadshaug, Larry Burke of Outside, Keith and Antjie Gunnar, Phil Clement, John Ball, Mike Cisler, Jan Edmondson, Mike Egeck, John Horvers, Terry Heckler, Gordon Bowker, Walt Mullen, Dan McConnell, John McEuen, Cori Nickerson, Craig Westlin, Jim Wickwire, John Roskelly, Kim Vanderhyden, and the Spalding family—each of you know why you're special to me.

I'd like to thank Ed Viesturs who is a climber extraordinaire and JanSport athlete.

Nawang Gombu and Pershumba Sherpa are great friends and adventurers.

Mike DeYoung contributed his amazing graphic talents.

Thanks also to the Collegiate team and sales reps of this vital division of JanSport.

Last but not least, I would like to thank Ted Eugenes, Mike Stroud, Jim Whittaker, Gombu the dog, and Jeff Weidman.

и и и

The year of 2005 is one I will never forget. My wife Winnie and I moved from Wisconsin to the San Francisco area where JanSport's corporate office was being relocated. That fall, I signed a contract with NAKED INK to write this book. A month later, I found out that I had a cancerous tumor on my lower right lung that would have to be removed. Talk about a mountain to climb.

My surgeon, Dr. Aguirre, owns a small winery in Livermore, and since one of my passions is gardening and growing vegetables, I knew I would be in good hands. He provided the successful surgery and, as extra insurance, I did chemo for three months. A special thanks goes to Dr. Aguirre, Dr. Wong, Kris, Suzanne, and Dr. Szumowski in Chemo at Valley Care. The support of my family, friends, and JanSport gave me the strength and the will to maintain a positive attitude as I walked through this experience.

In addition to thanking these key contributors to my story, allow me to leave you with these thoughts: Life is a gift. Live life to the fullest. Enjoy every moment. Don't be afraid to do what you want to do. And, I'd especially encourage young people to exercise social and environmental responsibility as they get out and explore the Earth.

Life is an adventure and the path is unknown; follow your dreams.

JANSPORT:

A VERY GROOVY HISTORY

Founded on the principle of getting out and discovering life for yourself, JanSport has continuously broken down barriers in the personal carrying device industry and continues to do so today.

At its inception, JanSport's three founders were called "a buncha long-haired hippies that spent too much time above the tree line." But with the long hair and the floral bells came ideas. Ideas that became a reality by the three discovering adventure for themselves—not reading about it in a book.

The history of JanSport plays out like a movie script—with one exception. This movie has been playing for forty years, and the phrase "The End" is not in our vocabulary.

1967

The award for what? After designing a flexible aluminum frame for an Alcoa Aluminum contest, Murray Pletz won the award for best design. With his winnings and the help of cousin Skip Yowell and girlfriend Jan Lewis, he started a small frame pack company in Seattle, Washington.

What one does for love. Engagement rings are one thing, but Murray took it a step further, promising his girlfriend Jan to name the company after her if she would marry him. We believe you can figure out what her answer was.

Ahh, the smell of transmission fluid in the morning. The first JanSport production site was the upstairs of Murray's dad's transmission shop in North Seattle. At this point, the quality was in the product and certainly not the surroundings.

Sharing the wealth (well, none yet really) with the family. With money still tight, Skip, Jan, and Murray depended on help from their families. Skip's aunt Mable did the company books and father Harold and uncle Norm made and maintained the aluminum frame benders.

215

1968-1970

The capital of climbing: Seattle, WA. In a retail store the size of Skip's current office (no joke), JanSport sold specialty packs to climbers that came to the Seattle area for the landscape. JanSport provided a specialized technical pack to these climbers that they had never seen before.

A pack for Spot? With climbers came sales, but also came dogs. Yes, in the early 70s they designed packs for the climbers' dogs so they too could conquer the North Cascades in comfort.

Friendship at 14,000 feet. In the early 70s, Lou Whittaker ran a small ski shop in Tacoma, WA. He was one of JanSport's early customers and helped popularize their technical packs in the Tacoma area. Lou also owned Rainier Mountaineers Inc. (RMI), a guide service in Mt. Rainier National Park. When Skip and Murray caught wind of a trip going up Rainier (Lou's first winter seminar in 1971), they figured what better time to do a little PR for JanSport. As it would figure, this was the first time the two tried climbing Rainier and this was the year the mountain had a record snowfall—1,122 inches. After being led out by Lou, JanSport asked him to sign on as an equipment tester and promotional consultant. Lou and the rest of the RMI team are still our testers today and we wouldn't have it any other way.

A one-of-a-kind pack becomes a JanSport regular. Originally designing the pack specifically for a customer, the benefits of a panel loading pack soon became apparent. The panel loading system plus padded hipbelt and adjustable frame was a great alternative to the standard top loading rucksacks of the day.

A thank you to the Huskies. A small sports shop in the off-campus bookstore of the University of Washington turned out to be a launching pad for the JanSport daypack business as we know it today. The shop purchased a few of JanSport's cross-country ski packs (the Ski n' Hike) and sold them quickly. Because of Seattle's world-renowned rainfall, students were actually buying the packs to carry their books and keep them somewhat dry. The Ski N' Hike inadvertently proved to be the first JanSport bookbag.

1971

Living in Tahiti and sipping drinks on the beach. Well, that's what could've happened if the idea was patented. After a trip to the Cascades that proved to be a bit too rough for comfort, Skip, Murray, and Jan returned to Seattle with a plan. Design a tent based on how Eskimos have designed their igloos for hundreds of years. The dome tent was created and became a sensation across the country—opening the floodgates for other JanSport product to enter retail channels.

A friend from the other side of the world. While climbing at Mt. Rainier in the Summer of 1971, Skip befriended Nawang Gombu, a guide for RMI. More importantly however, Gombu was the first person in the world to summit Mt. Everest twice. Skip and Gombu have had a long standing friendship and talk more about pleasure than business these days.

K2 Ski Company purchases JanSport. We move from our North Seattle transmission shop north to Paine Field in Everett, Washington. JanSport sets up its new headquarters in an old Air Force Barracks—paying $.03/square foot for rent.

JanSport goes Hollywood. (This is no six degrees of Kevin Bacon.) While making the movie *Idaho Transfer*, actor Peter Fonda ended up taping some scenes in Redmond, Washington near the JanSport gang. Taking inspiration from his patriotic bike in *Easy Rider*, JanSport designed the "Captain America" pack to show Fonda. The pack was a hit on set and proved to be just as popular with the public.

1972

JanSport sittin' on top of the world (or at least close to it). The first design of the timeless D-Series packs was specifically produced for a Dhaulagiris expedition led by Rainier guide Ron Fear in the Himalayas. Both parties benefited as the climbers summited and JanSport gained invaluable feedback on their D-Series packs.

1973

International exposure in the oddest of places. A college student, Peter Jenkins, ended up on the steps of the *National Geographic* offices. He was dissatisfied with our country, but following the advice of a school janitor, decided to travel the nation

217

see what it was worth. Obviously a man walking across America was a great story, so *National Geographic* gave him film and a camera to document his adventures. Some time through the trip, Jenkins gear had worn out. Remembering a classic JanSport ad he'd seen in an outdoor shop back home, he contacted JanSport for a gear donation. Skip was floored by the story and sent the gear. That gear made its way to the cover of *National Geographic* that year. JanSport and Skip were also mentioned in Jenkins' book telling of his trip. The book *Walk Across America* became an immediate fixture on the *New York Times* Best Seller's list and even became required reading for students in the state of Indiana.

As Lou Whittaker was organizing an expedition to Tibet, this time it was Skip who called on Jenkins. With no hesitation, Jenkins went with and documented JanSport's expedition across China to Tibet entitling it *Across China*.

1974

Becoming legit—one pack at a time. A major landmark was reached in minimal years for JanSport. Quality technical packs and increasingly popular daypacks helped bolster sales to the $1 million mark making JanSport a major player in the young outdoor industry.

Giving back to the retailers. The outdoors and more importantly, Mt. Rainier served as inspiration for the JanSport brand. So, what better way to thank retailers for carrying our product than a trip to the Great Northwest? The annual Mt. Rainier dealer climb is JanSport's way of passing the "experience junkie" mindset onto our retailers and is a tradition that continues today.

Convertible pack for the hills or hostels. With the newly discovered college market in mind, JanSport developed a convertible pack to be carried as either luggage or a backpack for trips. The pack's features would come in handy as travelers were hopping a bus or hiking a trail. Wherever they ended up it would hold up, as each design was tested atop Rainier just as most JanSport products.

From one trailblazer to another. Prior to JanSport, Skip read a book entitled *Seven Arrows* that discussed the importance of nature in the philosophy of some Midwest Indian tribes. Motivated by this book, he co-designed a logo with the help of Dan and Jill Anderson called "Four Great Directions." It symbolizes strength of character and adventurous spirit. Every year or so, Skip hands out a handmade "Four Great Directions" pin to an individual whose character and actions run consistent with *Seven Arrows*.

1977

219

Sign him up—he's good. On the 1977 Rainier climb, JanSport first got introduced to Ed Viesturs, an RMI guide and mountaineering phenom at the time. Through product testing and technical feedback, Ed and JanSport became working partners. Who knew that the relationship forged would lead to JanSport packs reaching many of Ed's 8,000 meter peaks without oxygen?

1982

Joining forces with a clothier. JanSport, a backpack company from Washington, and Downers, an active wear company from Wisconsin, saw fit to connect. An unlikely match up? Seems so. But the meshing of the two companies has proven to be a runaway success. Downers, now JanSport's Collegiate Division, catered to the college market with custom sportswear. The bookstore connections of Downers nationwide helped JanSport increase its daypack popularity amongst students.

JanSport sponsorships proves worthy. In 1982 and 1984, JanSport supported and sponsored two China-Everest Expeditions lead by longtime friend Lou Whittaker. Both were documented for PBS (*Everest North Wall* and *Winds of Everest*) and still air on the channel today. The films added to JanSport's already established credibility in the outdoor industry.

1984-1986

JanSport bought and then sold and then bought again. Starting with a court battle over a product name and ending in a purchase of the company, JanSport became part of the VF Corporation, the world's largest apparel company. Although JanSport became part of "Corporate America, our casual JanSport values remain intact.

1985

Over one million served. What was once an exclusive club had now officially turned into a phenomenon. JanSport tops the 1,000,000 daypacks sold milestone.

1989

Can you say Kangchenjunga? JanSport sponsored and fully equipped an expedition to the third highest peak in the world. After three months and four members dropping out, six others summited Kangchenjunga. This was the first time this was accomplished by an American team—and JanSport was on their backs the whole way up.

1990

An icon for generations. What once began as a contest entry has now become the most popular backpack brand in the world. JanSport are the packs that travel with their owners from home to school, country to country, and generation to generation.

1993

Where the Water Buffalo roam. Skip and the JanSport team invite friends and retailers to join them on Mt. Kilimanjaro. The traverse of Kilimanjaro adds another notch in the belt of JanSport climbs, with a week in Masai Mara viewing wildlife and celebration on the coast of Mombasa.

1992

JanSport turns 25 (yet parties like an 18-year-old). For our 25th birthday, a signed, limited edition painting was commissioned illustrating focal points of JanSport's first 25 years. This was also the year where the Annual Shake n' Bake party at the Outdoor Retailer Trade Show bypassed nuts and headed straight to crazy (due in part to John McEuen of the Nitty Gritty Dirt Band).

1995

One big, happy family. The international headquarters became official as all of JanSport's operations—besides warranty service and warehousing—joined forces in Appleton, Wisconsin in a new 212,000 square foot facility. We knew it was official once Skip and Jan rented the moving trucks.

A climb for cancer. JanSport helps organize, sponsor, and raise funds for *Expedition Inspiration*. The climb featured seventeen breast cancer survivors that summited Mt. Aconcogua, the highest peak in the Western Hemisphere, all in hopes to raise awareness and funds for breast cancer.

A little diversification never hurts. From wallets to shower kits, a line of travel accessories is introduced to blend with our packs and luggage. They are a hit with consumers as they realize the quality that comes with the JanSport tag.

JanSport blazes the trail to the world wide web. www.jansport.com officially debuts. Not only does the site provide company information to those who want it, but also acts as a virtual catalog offering the latest and greatest about JanSport packs and where to find them.

JanSport allowed into Bhutan. With the help of longtime friend Nawang Gombu, Skip and seven others got permits to trek through the very private country of Bhutan. Trading stamps with the locals, visiting the Tiger's Nest monastery, and climbing in the Himalayas helped us further realize the importance of getting out and discovering.

1996

Time for a passport. The company further spreads its wings opening an office in London and in Hong Kong. JanSport Europe and Asia are born.

JanSport forges relationship with a grand cause. JanSport begins support of Big City Mountaineers (BCM) through both financial means and volunteers. BCM is unique in that it allows young teens from disadvantaged, urban backgrounds to go out and experience landscape that they would've never seen. Many JanSport employees have participated in this program, and Skip is going on his fifth trip this summer.

1997

What do Travis Barker, Pink, and Jonny Mosely have in common? Trailblazing newcomers from the worlds of film, music, and sports combined with the hottest JanSport backpacks is a recipe for success. And that's exactly what the "Back Pack" print ad campaign received. Audiences left every retailer turned upside down in search of the JanSport *Velocity,* a.k.a the "Pink" back-pack. Sorry, they're still on back order.

A partnership with a worthy educational program. Believing in the same values and ethics that our company was founded on, JanSport proudly becomes a Principal Partner with the *Leave No Trace* Educational Program.

1999

Airlift has landed. The never-stagnant JanSport design team outdid themselves with the Airlift strap. Coined as the "world's most comfortable shoulder strap," the Airlift features impact absorbing Gelastic Gellycomb wrapped in a layer of dual density foam. Ironically, since 1999, average GPA scores amongst high schoolers has soared . . . a coincidence?

A moral obligation to our consumers. A full list of not only manufacturing sites but also contractors is disclosed to show JanSport's commitment to ethical and safe working conditions. JanSport also adopts the code of conduct per the *Fair Labor Association* (FLA).

2000

Competition becomes family. JanSport's largest competitor Eastpak® was acquired in 1999. Eastpak® enjoys great success in Europe while JanSport keeps its loyal fan base in the States.

Thinking outside the box. Feedback from female consumers found that they loved their JanSport packs so much they wish they could transfer our quality to their other bags. This motivated the creation of our first Lifestyle line, a collection of shoulder bags and crossover packs created specifically for fashion conscious women who want the JanSport label over their shoulder.

Helping conserve America's natural wonders. JanSport becomes a supporter of the *Continental Divide Trail Alliance*—a non-profit whose hopes are to complete a 3,100 mile trail running south from Canada to Mexico, passing through five states along the way.

2001

Technical packs built for any and all. We segmented our technical pack category into three areas: Freedom, Backcountry, and Pro. This helps the consumer pick a pack that best suits them so they won't end up with too little or too much pack. The Women's Specific technical line also debuts.

2002

Luggage doesn't have to be square. JanSport's unique Active Travel line gives a new definition to luggage. The line is designed to be rugged enough for the adventurer or refined enough for the jetsetter.

2003

The hydration combination. JanSport and Nalgene™ join forces with two top-end hydration systems: the Water Tower and the Hydro Dynamic.

2005

An athlete on Annapurna. JanSport athlete Ed Viesturs summits Annapurna massif without supplementary oxygen. Situated in North-central Nepal, its 26,545 feet (8,091 meters) makes Annapurna the world's tenth highest mountain. To date, Viesturs has stood on the summit of the world's fourteen highest mountains—all without oxygen—and with us on his back. We're sure he breathes easier knowing that his favorite JanSport technical pack is still in stock.

Go West, young man. JanSport gets a new home by relocating the corporate offices to San Leandro, California. Skip is happy because he's now closer to the heart of wine country, his daughter Quinn, and favorite granddaughter Drew.

2006

Mountain legend and longtime friend Peter Whittaker became an official JanSport athlete. Peter participated in the China-Everest climb of 1984. His experience and expertise make him the perfect spokesman for JanSport's line of Pro packs.

JanSport takes the "yawn" out of luggage. With the all new SuperBreak® Travel Collection, infused with more fun than a travel bag has ever known, this mix-and-match line features duffels, totes, uprights and business cases in groovy colors and patterns sure to be the envy of baggage handlers everywhere.

Hippies unite! Whoever said that hippies would never conquer the world obviously underestimated the spirit of JanSport. With its expansion into Europe and with the opening of its first store in Chile, JanSport continues to explore the ends of the earth in style while remaining the industry leader.

. . . and the beat goes on.